THE BIBLE IN THE BOWLS

THE BIBLE IN THE BOWLS

A Catalogue of Biblical Quotations in Published Jewish Babylonian Aramaic Magic Bowls

Daniel James Waller

With a contribution from
Dorota Molin

https://www.openbookpublishers.com

© 2022 Daniel James Waller, with a contribution from Dorota Molin.

This work is licensed under a Creative Commons Attribution-NonCommercial 4.0 International (CC BY-NC 4.0). This license allows you to share, copy, distribute and transmit the text; to adapt the text for non-commercial purposes of the text providing attribution is made to the authors (but not in any way that suggests that they endorse you or your use of the work). Attribution should include the following information:

Daniel James Waller, *The Bible in the Bowls: A Catalogue of Biblical Quotations in Published Jewish Babylonian Aramaic Magic Bowls*. Cambridge Semitic Languages and Cultures 16. Cambridge, UK: Open Book Publishers, 2022, https://doi.org/10.11647/OBP.0305

Copyright and permissions for the reuse of many of the images included in this publication differ from the above. Copyright and permissions information for images is provided separately in the List of Illustrations.

Further details about CC BY-NC licenses are available at, https://creativecommons.org/licenses/by-nc/4.0/

All external links were active at the time of publication unless otherwise stated and have been archived via the Internet Archive Wayback Machine at https://archive.org/web

Updated digital material and resources associated with this volume are available at https://doi.org/10.11647/OBP.0305#resources

Every effort has been made to identify and contact copyright holders and any omission or error will be corrected if notification is made to the publisher.

Semitic Languages and Cultures 16.

ISSN (print): 2632-6906
ISSN (digital): 2632-6914

ISBN Paperback: 9781800647633
ISBN Hardback: 9781800647640
ISBN Digital (PDF): 9781800647657
DOI: 10.11647/OBP.0305

Cover images: Museu da Farmácia, Lisbon

Cover design: Jeevanjot Kaur Nagpal

CONTENTS

Preface vii

Introduction 1

   1.0.   Quotation and Allusion   8

   2.0.   The Form and Uses of the Biblical
                Quotations in the Bowls 12

       2.1.   The Form of the Quotations 13

       2.2.   The Uses of the Quotations 18

            2.2.1.   Prophylactics and Apotropaics 23

            2.2.2.   Curative Uses 24

            2.2.3.   For Popularity and Success 27

            2.2.4.   Aggressive Uses 28

   3.0.   The Orthography of the Quotations in the
                Context of Late Antique Bible Transmission 30

   4.0.   Reconstructing the Language behind the
                Quotations 34

   5.0.   Note on the Transcription of Bowl Texts 39

Catalogue of Biblical Quotations in Published
Jewish Babylonian Aramaic Magic Bowls 41

   1.0.   Note on the Catalogue 41

   2.0.   Abbreviations and Symbols 42

3.0. Sigla 44

4.0. Reference Guide to Bowl Texts 44

5.0. Catalogue of Biblical Quotations 46

Table Showing the Distribution of Biblical
Quotations in Published JBA Incantation Bowls 153

Bibliography 163

Ancient Sources Index 181

PREFACE

The Jewish Babylonian Aramaic incantation bowls represent our only significant corpus of direct epigraphic documents from late antique Mesopotamia written by that region's Jewish communities. They are of immense importance for our understanding of these communities, and scholarship has increasingly come to recognise just how far these previously marginalised artefacts may lead to new perceptions of ancient Jewish society. As of November 2022, over 460 Jewish Babylonian Aramaic bowls have been published in widely scattered editions of varying quality, a circumstance that impedes the systematic study of various aspects of the bowl texts, including their extensive quotation of the Hebrew Bible. The present work collates all of the biblical quotations found in these disparate publications.

By making these quotations easily accessible to scholars, this catalogue is designed to facilitate research not just by students of Jewish magic, but by linguists, liturgists, biblical text critics, and historians. It will hopefully aid and accelerate further research on the use and dynamics of scriptural citation in the magic bowls and ancient Jewish magic more broadly; on the social locations of biblical knowledge in the Jewish communities of Sasanian Mesopotamia; on the formation of the liturgy and the development of the Jewish prayer book; on the transmission of biblical texts in late antiquity and the phonology and morphology of the Babylonian reading tradition; and in the area of biblical text criticism, as some bowl texts contain the earliest attestations of biblical passages not found in the Dead Sea Scrolls.

© 2022 Waller and Molin, CC BY-NC 4.0   https://doi.org/10.11647/OBP.0305.04

The publication of bowl texts is an ongoing process, and unpublished bowl texts currently outnumber published bowl texts. The number of biblical quotations known from the bowls will thus continue to grow. As such—and given the possibilities afforded by publication in this series—it is my intention to periodically update this catalogue as editions of new bowl texts appear. In its current form, the present work represents a complete catalogue of biblical quotations from the corpus of Jewish Babylonian Aramaic bowls published as of November 2022.

Finally, it is my great pleasure to thank Dorota Molin for her contribution to §§3.0 and 4.0 of the introduction to the catalogue and for her help with several other aspects of the catalogue. I would also like to thank Hindy Najman for her generous encouragement and support; Siam Bhayro for his assistance; and Geoffrey Khan and Aaron Hornkohl for their patience with the technical aspects of the catalogue. I am also indebted to the anonymous reviewers of the manuscript for their helpful comments, and for a meticulous reading of the catalogue. Work on the catalogue was made possible by funding from the Niels Stensen Fellowship and was completed while I was a Visiting Scholar of the Centre for Hebrew and Jewish Studies of the University of Oxford.

Daniel James Waller

I thank Geoffrey Khan for introducing me to the incantation bowls and for his support in my study of the Babylonian Hebrew pronunciation tradition.

Dorota Molin

INTRODUCTION

with Dorota Molin

Late antique Mesopotamia was a dangerous place. It was populated by a true rogues' gallery of demons, who were participants in—and often the principal cause of—domestic crises, disease, and various other misfortunes. Curses, sorcery, and other forms of human malice were also a common threat. In light of this menacing reality, large numbers of people availed themselves of the objects that we now refer to as magic bowls or incantation bowls.[1] These reflect a largely apotropaic practice, whereby protective spells were written on the inside of unglazed earthenware bowls. Once inscribed, the bowls were turned upside down and placed under thresholds or buried beneath the floors of people's homes. There they worked to 'press', trap, or expel demons, or to ward off the potential threat of demons, evil sorcery, and other (demonised and/or personified) forms of human malice.

Magic bowls have been discovered since the middle of the nineteenth century in excavations around Mesopotamia, while the large majority of provenanced bowls derive from a number

---

[1] For more substantial overviews of this striking body of magico-religious objects from Sasanian Mesopotamia, see either Bohak (2008, 183–193) or Harari (2017, 234–251).

of sites in central Iraq.² Several unpublished incantation bowls are inscribed with Seleucid calendar dates in accordance with the conventions of legal documents. These dates correspond to 545, 573/4, 580, and 611 CE (Shaked et al. 2013, 1). We thus possess positive evidence for the production of magic bowls during the sixth and seventh centuries. The practice of inscribing bowls presumably began earlier, possibly even in the fourth century, and came to an end towards the end of the seventh century or shortly thereafter.

The spells on the large majority of these objects were inscribed by Babylonian Jews using the Aramaic square script.³ For the most part, they are composed in an archaic literary form of Jewish Babylonian Aramaic (JBA).⁴ The language of these spells lacks homogeneity from a linguistic point of view, however, and cannot be simply or easily generalised. Nonetheless, the archaic dialect(s) of JBA used in the bowls appears to have differed significantly from the spoken language of contemporary Babylonian Jews, though vernacular JBA remains the prime suspect in cases of linguistic interference in both the Aramaic and Hebrew strata of the bowl texts.

---

² For a partial snapshot of various locations where magic bowls have been discovered, see the map in Müller-Kessler (2017).

³ Other bowls written in Syriac and Mandaic were produced by members of neighbouring communities in Sasanian Mesopotamia.

⁴ This consensus view is reflected, e.g., in Rossell (1953, 11), Juusola (1999, 247–250), and Ford 2012 (215). See the contribution by Morgenstern to Shaked et al. (2013, 39–49) for a snapshot of the linguistic situation in the JBA bowl texts.

The crux of most bowl texts is the moment of adjuration, where demons are made to desist from harming the bowl owner or are put to flight using various bans, anathemas, or divorce formulae. The authority and legitimacy of these pronouncements was naturally of great concern to the bowl writers. As such, they marshalled a variety of peremptory techniques—open neither to appeal nor to challenge—designed to augment the authority of their injunctions. Most commonly, the bowl writers stated themselves to be acting in the name of God, to whom all things are, of course, subject. They also deployed various and occasionally arcane divine epithets and names of power. Appeals to angels on behalf of the bowl owners were also common, as was the use of binding legal formulae and invocations of powerful biblical and rabbinic figures.

A number of magic bowls also quote scriptural verses in support of their goals, and the present work comprises a complete catalogue of quotations from the Hebrew Bible contained in the published corpus of JBA bowls.[5] The parameters with respect to the Hebrew Bible are based on the consonantal Masoretic Text (MT) as represented by the Leningrad Codex (I Firkovitch B19A). The catalogue also includes a number of *targumim*. Some 464 (largely) legible and comprehensible JBA magic bowls have been

---

[5] Several biblical verses from unpublished bowls in the Schøyen collection are quoted in the introduction to Shaked et al. (2013, 19–20). These are not included in the present catalogue. Further to this, a number of biblical quotations in unpublished JBA bowls in the Vorderasiatisches Museum are noted, but not transcribed, in the descriptive catalogue of this collection in Bhayro et al. (2018).

published since 1853 in diverse and widely scattered editions of varying quality, a circumstance that impedes the systematic study of various aspects of their texts. By collating the biblical quotations found in these disparate publications and making them easily accessible, I hope to facilitate further work in several sometimes-related areas:

(1) The use and dynamics of scriptural citation in the magic bowls and Jewish magical texts more broadly.[6]

(2) The socio-religious typology of the bowls, the social locations of biblical knowledge in late antique Babylonia, and the

---

[6] Discussions of scriptural citation in the bowls are largely confined to smaller observations within commentaries on published texts. There are several exceptions, however. Polzer (1986) represents an extensive survey of biblical citation in the bowls, but her starting corpus consisted of only 105 bowl texts and her valuable study has been rendered somewhat out-of-date by the relative explosion in the publication of bowl texts since the 1980s. More recently, Müller-Kessler (2013) has provided a detailed survey of biblical quotations from 59 published bowls; Lanfer (2015) has assessed the value of the bowl texts for the study of the Hebrew Bible; Korsvoll (2018) has surveyed the distribution of biblical quotations across several major corpora of bowl texts; and Bhayro (2021) has studied quotations from the Psalms in the bowl texts. For general remarks on the Bible in the bowls, see Levene (2003, 10–14) and Shaked et al. (2013, 18–20). On the use of the Bible in Jewish magic more broadly, see Bohak (2008, 308–14) and Angel (2009). For surveys of the biblical verses used in both ancient and medieval Jewish magic, see Schiffman and Swartz (1992, 37–42) and Naveh and Shaked (1993, 22–31). An extensive survey and treatment of the biblical quotations and allusions in the Hebrew and Aramaic magical texts from the Cairo Genizah is to be found in Salzer (2010). The present catalogue is designed as a complement to that work.

different ways in which bowl writers encountered scripture, whether in the context of the liturgy or through other encounters with oral or written scripture, such as its reproduction in scribal milieux.[7] A number of the bowl texts that contain biblical quotations also contain overt allusions to biblical figures and stories, as well as other explicit indicators of (deep) familiarity with the Jewish literary traditions of late antiquity, including rabbinic and Hekhalot literature. The JBA bowls are far from a homogeneous corpus, and the increasing correlation of such types of uniquely 'Jewish' spell contents (scriptural and otherwise) with a typology of the (scribal) hands behind the bowl texts will likely permit more specific insights into the immediate professional milieux of some bowl writers, their repertoires, and the social locations of biblical and other forms of knowledge.[8] This should prove of great value not just for socio-religious typologies of the bowls, but also for our understanding of the diversity of Jewish society in Sasanian Mesopotamia.[9]

(3) The oral modes of transmission of the biblical text in late antiquity, the reproduction of scripture from aural memory,

---

[7] For evidence that some bowl writers worked as professional scribes, see Bhayro (2015) and Manekin-Bamberger (2015; 2020).
[8] In this respect, see the important discussions in Manekin-Bamberger (2020) and Gross and Manekin-Bamberger (2022).
[9] For initial sociological syntheses of the bowl texts and their implications for our understanding of Sasanian Mesopotamia and its (important minority) communities, see Morony (2003) and Herman (2019; 2021, 131–36).

the phonology and morphology of the Babylonian reading tradition, and the potential interference of contact languages on this reading tradition.[10]

(4) The formation of the liturgy and the development of the Jewish prayer book. A large proportion of the biblical quotations in the bowl texts were known then or later in liturgical contexts, while specific combinations of scripture in the bowls are often consistent with liturgical formulae.[11] Their use may have been stimulated in part by this liturgical usage and not just their appearance in scripture alone.[12] Further to this, some bowls may bear witness to early stages in the development of the liturgy. The bowl M 108 (Levene 2003, 71), for instance, quotes a combination of verses (Pss 89.53; 106.48; 72.18–19; 104.31; 106.47) that parallels the communal response prescribed in the fourth section of the ʿArvit in Seder ʿAmram.[13] This prayer is attributed by ʿAmram Gaon to the "later rabbis" (i.e., the post-Talmudic or Saboraic rabbis of the sixth to seventh centuries). This would not

---

[10] For recent research in these areas, see Abudraham (2020), Frim (2021), and Molin (2017; 2020). Cf. the pioneering study of Hebrew in the bowls by Mishor (2007), as well as Elitzur (2013).

[11] On Jewish liturgy and the bowl texts, see Naveh and Shaked (1993, 22–31) and Levene (2003, 11–14; 2005). On magic and liturgy more broadly, see Schäfer (1996) and van der Vliet (2011).

[12] An excellent example is provided by a pair of duplicate bowls (VA 3853 and VA 3854) in Levene (2003) that do not just quote the first two groups of verses from the Shemaʿ (Deut. 6.4–9 and 11.13–21), but include the liturgical response ברוך שם כבוד מלכותו לעולם ועד 'Blessed is the name of His glorious kingdom forever' at the appropriate point in the quotation.

[13] See Levene (2005, 173–74) for further discussion.

just make M 108 the oldest witness to this prayer; it would also reflect the use in a magic bowl of a prayer that had only recently been introduced.

(5) Biblical text criticism. Textual critics often neglect texts, like amulets and magic bowls, that contain non-continuous portions of scripture, though some bowl texts contain the earliest attestations of biblical passages not found in the Dead Sea Scrolls or elsewhere in the Judaean desert; they thus possess text-critical value in studies of the transmission history of the Hebrew Bible.[14]

The remainder of this introduction serves several purposes. In the first place, it defines quotation for the purposes of the catalogue. It then provides a number of initial observations about the form and the use of the biblical quotations in the bowls. This is followed by some discussion of the orthography of the quotations in the context of late antique biblical transmission and the value of these spellings for reconstructing the extant Hebrew pronunciation traditions of late antique Babylonia. This discussion also considers the extent to which the biblical quotations in the bowls originated in liturgical practice—whether prayer or public reading of the weekly Torah portion—or in a written tradition of Biblical Hebrew.

---

[14] See Pickering (1999) and Lanfer (2015). Similarly, as Herman (2021, 133) points out, quotations from rabbinic literature in the bowl spells "can even contribute towards establishing the most accurate original text within the Talmud."

1.0. Quotation and Allusion

The practice of incorporating earlier spoken or written materials into the body of a later composition is frequent in literature of all times, but there is considerable disagreement in comparative literary theory regarding the nature of quotation and allusion, as well as little scholarly consensus on the terminology and methodology to be used in treating them. By all accounts, the category of quotation includes at least some ways of reporting or repeating the actual speech or discourse of someone else, while many scholars differentiate between quotation and allusion on this basis: that quotation is the direct use of a prior text and allusion an indirect use of a prior text. But the realities of quotation in the ancient world are complex, and it can sometimes be difficult to say what constitutes the repetition of discourse in a world of non-standardised texts where the accurate reproduction of the actual words of an earlier text—let alone the acknowledgment of this reproduction using an explicit citation formula—does not appear to have always been a priority.

For the purposes of this catalogue, I use the term quotation to refer not to exact reproductions of the orthography of the MT or the *targumim* in the bowls, but—allowing for orthographic variance—to a marked formal correspondence or sustained lexical linkage with the actual words of an antecedent scriptural text.[15] The term 'pseudo-quotation' is thus reserved for phenomena like

---

[15] The scriptural quotations in the bowls agree with the Masoretic orthography to varying degrees. Divergences generally reflect phonetic spellings and the reproduction of biblical texts from memory. See §§3.0 and 4.0 below.

conflation or paraphrase. Such marked formal correspondences can be easily observed between a variety of biblical texts and portions of the bowl texts in 130 published bowls.[16] Though only some of these quotations are explicitly marked with an introduction or citation formula as the words of someone else, they are all obviously (intended to be) quotations. And even though 'sustained lexical linkage' is a fairly loose stipulation, it nevertheless accomplishes a sharp distinction between quotation and other forms of biblical citation in the bowls. Only rarely does a marginal instance creep into the catalogue. A good example is a pseudo-quotation that appears in the bowl AMB 9:5–6 (Naveh and Shaked 1987, 174–76). Even though this passage represents at best a conflation and paraphrase of several biblical verses, it is included because it is preceded by an explicit citation formula (just like nine other recognisable biblical quotations in the same bowl text).

In any case, it is simply impossible to remove a certain element of subjectivity from such an endeavour, especially when

---

[16] In one rare instance, a quotation of Ps. 115.1 begins in Hebrew, but continues in a *targum* which is not identical to any *targum* known to us; see Shaked (2015, 109–10). In this case, we have an instance of quotation that problematises the notion of quotation as a formal correspondence between the words of a manifest text and the words of an antecedent text; the difficulty here is our inability to identify the specific prior text, though this difficulty is smoothed over by the initial Hebrew. See below for discussion of other marginal instances.

approaching the blurry border line between quotation and allusion.[17] A good example is the use of Isa. 45.2b in the bowl M 155:6–7 (Levene 2003, 110–15). The bowl text calls upon Gabriel, Michael, and Raphael—who are said in the bowl text to shatter copper doors and cut iron bars, just like God promised to do for Cyrus in the book of Isaiah—to shatter and cut off an evil spirit.

M 155:6–7   על ידי גבריאל ומיכאל ורפאל די מתברין דלתות
נחושא וימגדעין בריחי ברזל אינון יתברון ויגדעון
לרוחא בישתא

Isa. 45.2b   דלתות נחושה אשבר ובריחי ברזל אגדע

The bowl text retains parts of the Hebrew original (דלתות נחושא and בריחי ברזל and the verb גדע), though the conjugation of the verbs is adapted and שבר is replaced with תבר. An argument could

---

[17] The concept of allusion is especially difficult to define and—more so than quotation—is complicated by questions of authorial intent and the fact that no two readers are likely to perceive brief parallels between any texts in the same way. Numerous scholars using different (theoretical) frameworks have sought to establish formal principles for the description and classification of allusions, as well as to establish how allusion comes into being and where it exists (in the text, in the author's mind, or in the mind of the reader). By most accounts, allusion is a way of signifying where some kind of overt or covert marker is used to both denote an earlier text and recover one or more properties of this earlier text in order to modify a later text. The perception of generic affinity is thus the driving force of allusion; it is what directs the reader to a particular interpretation of the later text. These affinities may be simple or complex, and triggered by more or less overt markers. The JBA bowl texts are replete with overt allusions to the Hebrew Bible and other Jewish literary traditions.

be made that this citation of Isa. 45.2 should be designated an overt allusion, though I ultimately include it in the catalogue. As with a handful of other marginal instances, it is marked in the catalogue as a paraphrastic pseudo-quotation. In two other cases, where the lexical linkages between the bowl and scripture are very brief, the broader context of the incantation played a role in deciding whether or not to include the case in the catalogue. Thus the isolated appearance of the epithet יה גיבור in the bowl JBA 28:10 (Shaked et al. 2013, 162), which the editors suggest is "possibly an abbreviated quotation" of Ps. 24.8b (which reads יְהוָה גִּבּוֹר מִלְחָמָה), is not included in the catalogue, while the doxological phrase יהוה מלך יהוה מאלך יהוה ימלך לעולם ועד (which fuses phrases from Pss 10.16 and 93.1 with Exod. 15.18) is included in the catalogue because it is consistently clustered together with several other biblical quotations in the bowls in which it is quoted.

Certain divine epithets, such as צור עולמ(י)ם 'Eternal Rock' (cf. Isa. 26.4b), though no doubt of a biblical origin, are so well-attested as independent epithets across both the bowls and rabbinic literature that I do not include them as quotations in the catalogue. Similarly, the phrase יהוה צבאות שמו 'The LORD of Hosts is his name' appears in a number of bowls; it also appears at thirteen different points in the Hebrew Bible. Because it is not possible to determine from the bowl texts which (if any) of these biblical verses is being quoted, I do not include this phrase in the catalogue. Further to these remarks, I do not include uses of the divine name from Exod. 3.14 in the catalogue; although the catalogue elsewhere includes the deployment of (partial) quotations as (parts of) divine epithets in the bowls, the inclusion of this partial quotation from Exod. 3.14 and variations on it would have blown the catalogue up to a truly unwieldy size.

2.0. The Form and Uses of the Biblical Quotations in the Bowls

The JBA bowl texts quote from multiple books of the Bible.[18] As Korsvoll (2018, 90) has pointed out, however, biblical quotations in the bowl texts are neither ubiquitous nor are they evenly distributed across the corpus.[19] In fact, the majority of quotations cluster in a minority of bowls. Of the 464 bowl texts published thus far, 130 include quotations. Of these, 67 bowl texts feature

---

[18] Biblical books not represented in the bowl texts published thus far are Joshua, Judges, 2 Samuel, 1 Kings, Joel, Amos, Obadiah, Jonah, Nahum, Habakkuk, Zephaniah, Haggai, Malachi, Job, Ruth, Lamentations, Ecclesiastes, Esther, and Ezra. The books of Exodus, Numbers, Deuteronomy, Isaiah, and Psalms are particularly well represented in the published bowls, while Zech. 3.2 is, for reasons obvious in the context of the bowls, by far the most quoted single verse; quotations from Ps. 91 appear less often than might be expected given the apotropaic goals of many bowl texts.

[19] For example, of the thirty JBA/Hebrew bowls in the Hilprecht Sammlung recently re-edited by Ford and Morgenstern (2020), only 5 of 30 contain one or more quotations. Of the first tranche of bowls from the Schøyen Collection published by Shaked et al. (2013), only 19 of 64 contain quotations. Only 8 of 75 bowls in the collection of the British Museum published by Segal (2000) contain a quotation. Note that the readings in Segal (2000) are not always reliable, while Segal identifies a number of further scriptural citations in the British Museum bowls that are far from certain.

just one quotation, 26 feature two quotations, and 37 feature three or more quotations.[20] The table appended to the catalogue shows the distribution of biblical quotations across the published corpus of bowl texts.

Nonetheless, those bowls that contain quotations demonstrate the extensive scriptural knowledge of some bowl writers, while the interaction with scripture in these bowls affords us a vivid picture of the ways authoritative traditions were conceptualised and appropriated for apotropaic, exorcistic, curative, and (occasionally) aggressive purposes in the bowls. This section offers a brief overview of the form and use of biblical quotations in the bowl texts.

2.1. The Form of the Quotations

The form of the biblical quotations in the published bowls ranges from brief phrases to the entirety of individual biblical verses to the quotation of several continuous verses and even extended biblical passages. Müller-Kessler (2013, 227–228) has briefly distinguished three broad ways in which quotations are incorporated into the texts of bowls.

(1) Some bowl texts consist solely of biblical verses, though such texts are rare.[21] To these instances may be added bowls that

---

[20] Well over 2,000 magic bowls are known, and the number of quotations deriving from the published corpus thus reflects only a portion of the scriptural material in the bowl texts, as many unpublished texts include quotations.
[21] Examples of these are HS 3027 (Ford and Morgenstern 2020, 86–87), HS 3030 (Ford and Morgenstern 2020, 92–93), IM 141803 (Faraj 2010, 206–7), and A 33965 (Kaufman 1973).

largely abstain from an Aramaic incantation. An example is M 108 (Levene 2003, 71), the text of which consists of seven biblical verses and only a brief statement of purpose in Aramaic:

> הדין קמיעה למיסר שידי דיוי וסיוטי וסטני מן הדין ביתיה דאדיב בר בתשבתה

> This amulet is for the binding of demons, dēvs, and frights and satans from this house of Adib son of Bat-Šabbeta.

(2) Other bowl texts quote both partial and complete biblical verses as a fixed part of larger spell formulae. Examples of this phenomenon are the use of quotations as dialogue or character speech in various narrative spells. In a spell that recounts a meeting between the famous *tanna* Ḥanina ben Dosa and an evil spirit, for instance, the sage speaks to the demon and quotes Ps. 104.20 against her. A well-preserved example of this spell is to be found in JBA 9:7–9 (Shaked et al 2013, 79–81), which reads:

> מומינה עלכי ומשבענא עלכי אנתי רוחא בישתא דיפגע ביה ברבי חנינא בן דוסא ואמר לה רבי חנינא בן דוסא לרוחא בישתא דיפגע ביה בההיא שעתא קראה דיכתיב תשית חושך ויהי לילה בו תירמוס כל חיתו יאער

> I adjure you and I beswear you, you, evil spirit, who met Rabbi Ḥanina ben Dosa, and Rabbi Ḥanina ben Dosa said to her, to the evil spirit who met him at that time, the verse that is written: "'You make darkness and it is night, in which all beasts of the forest creep'" (Ps. 104.20).

Another example is the quotation of Isa. 40.12 in the popular Semamit historiola, where an evil agent known variously as Sideros and Sergi(u)s swears an oath not to harm the children of the bowl owner. He does so using the biblical verse as a divine epithet. Typically, only Isa. 40.12a is quoted by the evil agent, though the full verse is quoted in the version of the spell deployed in AMB 12b (Naveh and Shaked 1987, 189–193). The relevant part of the story reads:

> ואמר שבוקו מיני ואנא מישתבענא לכון במי שמדד בשועולו מים ושמים בזרת תיכן וכל בשליש עפר הארץ ושקל בפלס {ויגע} ויגבעות במואחנים דכל אתר דידכר שמיה דסיני וסאסיני וסינגרו וארתיקו איתרח{ם} (ס) ולא {אין} איחנוק ולא איקטול ליבנין דזבינו בר זוני ואינתתיה בת גוסי דאית להון וידהון להון מן יומא דנן ולעלם

> And he said, "Let go of me and I swear to you by the One 'who measured the waters in his palm and gauged the heavens with a span, and weighed <the mountains> with a scale and the hills with a balance' (Isa. 40.12) that wherever one mentions the name of Sini and Sasini and Sinigru and Artiqu, I shall have pity and shall not strangle or kill the children of Zabinu son of Zuni and his wife, daughter of Gusi, those whom they have and those whom they will have from this day to eternity."

Similarly, a bowl published by Shaked (2015, 109–110) recounts the pursuit of the Israelites by the Egyptians into the Sea of Reeds. In the bowl's telling of this story, Ps. 115.1 is placed into the mouths of the Egyptian charioteers as they realise they are about to perish at the hand of God:

> מומינא ומשבענא עלכי אנתי רוחא בישתא בשמיה דאלהא רבה ... דהוא נזף בימא ואיתרגישו כיפוהי כמה דיכתיב רוגע הים ויהמו גליו יהוה צבאות שמו {וע} כען אריס ליבהון מצראי לימא ורדפו בתר עמא לימא וברוגזה רבה איתגלי על ימא ורדפו בתר עמא לימא וברוגזא רבה איתגלי על ימא ואיתמסיאו מן קדמוהי ואמרו קדמוהי לא לנו יהוה לא לנו

> I adjure you and beswear you, you, the evil spirit, by the name of the great God ... who rebuked the sea and its banks shook, as it is written: 'I cleft the sea and its waves

roared, the LORD of Hosts is his name' (Isa. 51.15 = Jer. 31.34). Now He lifted the hearts of the Egyptians towards the sea and they pursued the people up to the sea, and He made an appearance with great wrath over the sea, and they pursued the people up to the sea, and He made an appearance with great wrath over the sea, and they dissolved from His presence, and said in His presence: "'Not to us, O LORD, not to us …'" (Ps. 115.1).

Strikingly, the quotation from Ps. 115 in this bowl, which begins in Hebrew, is continued in a hitherto unattested *targum* that embraces Ps. 115.1–2.

(3) Most bowl texts quote biblical verses not as a fixed part of spell formulae but as 'independent' units. These quotations sometimes open the bowl text or appear midway through the text. More commonly, they are to be found at (or towards) the end of the bowl text, where they sometimes cluster together. Polzer (1986, 107) has argued that this use of scripture—at the end of the incantation text and towards the rim of the bowl—may have been perceived to function as a kind of authoritative seal upon the text.[22] In other words, the scriptural verses were used to effect a kind of hedge around the edge of the bowl.[23]

---

[22] Bhayro (2021, 76) expands upon this observation and compares the possible use of biblical quotations in this respect to the common deployment of the scribal guarantee of effectiveness שריר וקים 'sound and established' to conclude some bowl texts.

[23] There was also undoubtedly a pragmatic aspect to the quotation of small units of scripture towards the end of the incantation text and the rim of the bowl: as the bowl writers neared the end of the writing space available to them on the inside of the bowl, it makes sense that they would have stuck to smaller units of text rather than launching into

Finally, biblical quotations sometimes appear in the bowl texts in emended form. The word order of quotations is occasionally inverted, or the verse is first written out forwards and then repeated backwards. Other bowl writers wove two separate biblical verses together by quoting alternating words from each verse, as with Deut. 6.4 and Ps. 91.1 in the bowl AMB 11:6–7 (Naveh and Shaked 1987, 184). The effect is as follows:

שמע יושב ישראל בסתר יהוה עליון אלהינו בצל יהוה שדי אחד יתלונן

Other forms of emendation include the insertion of the bowl owner's name directly into the biblical verse. In a bowl designed to cure a woman suffering from miscarriages, for example, the name of the beneficiary is inserted into Ps. 55.9 as follows:

אחישה {מיפלט} מיפלט למישכוי בת אנושפרי מרוח סועה מסער

> I would hasten escape *for Miškoy daughter of Anušfri* from the stormy wind and tempest.[24]

Occasionally, parts of a verse may be purposefully elided or omitted. A good example is the quotation of Num. 10.35 in a bowl designed to protect Mādar-Āfri daughter of Manušay against various forms of injurious magic. The verse is quoted in an unusual spelling with a telling alteration to the biblical text: the final five letters of משנאיך 'those who hate you' are deliberately omitted by the bowl writer:

ויהיי בין נסוע הארון וימר מושה קומא יהוה ויפוצו איבאך וינסו מ[vacat]
מיפנך

---

longer spell units that had the potential to spill over the rim of the bowl and onto its exterior (something they apparently sought to avoid).
[24] JBA 55:14 (Shaked et al. 2013, 246–247).

> And it happened, whenever the Ark set out, that Moses would say, 'Rise O LORD and let Your enemies scatter and let <those who hate You> flee before You!'²⁵

This alteration was undoubtedly intended as an act of sympathetic magic designed to excise and negate the threat of Mādar-Āfri's perceived enemies.

Some bowls also paraphrase or conflate biblical passages (whether intentionally or by accident) and I designate these particular instances pseudo-quotations. A good example is to be found in the bowl AMB 9:5–6 (Naveh and Shaked 1987, 174–176), where the 'quotation' is indicated using an explicit citation formula but in fact appears to be an allusion to or paraphrase of two different biblical verses:

> ויתקים עליה קראה דכתיב יפלו ולא י(ק)ומו ו(אל) תהה תקומא למפלתא
> ולא תהא אסותה למחתם

> May the following verse apply to him: "They shall fall and not arise (Jer. 8.4 or Amos 8.14) and there will be no power for them to stand (Lev. 26.37) after (their) downfall, and there will be no healing to their wound."

Finally, as briefly mentioned above, an occasional *targum* appears in the magic bowls. In these instances, the *targum* typically appears alongside the Hebrew verse. Very rarely, we encounter an Aramaic version without reference to the original Hebrew.

2.2. The Uses of the Quotations

Broadly speaking, the rationale behind the quotation of most biblical verses in the bowl texts is relatively easy to identify.

---

²⁵ AMB 3:5 (Naveh and Shaked 1987, 146).

(1) In many cases, the plain or literal sense of the quoted verse has an immediate bearing upon the stated aim of the incantation. For example, a rare instance of the genre of aggressive magic in the bowls quotes various verses from Deuteronomy and applies them to the intended victim of the bowl text:

> ותקים עליה על יהודה בר נני יככה ייי בשחפת ובקדחת ובדלקת ובחרחור ובחרב ובשידפון וב[ירקון] ורדפוך [עד אב]דך יככה ייי [בשחין ר]ע על הברכים ועל השוקים אשר לא {יו} יוכל להירפי מיכף רגלך ועד קודקודך [יכ]כה ייי בשיגעון ובעיורון וב[תמהון לבב]

> And may the following apply to Judah son of Nanay: "The LORD shall strike you with a wasting disease and with a fever and with an inflammation and with a fiery heat and with the sword and with blight and with [mildew] and they shall pursue you [until you per]ish" (Deut. 28.22). "The LORD shall strike you on the knees and on the legs with gr[ievous boils] of which you cannot be healed, from the sole of your foot to the crown of your head" (Deut. 28.35). "The LORD shall strike you with madness and with blindness and with [bewilderment of heart]" (Deut. 28.28).[26]

Here, the aims of the bowl are wholly congruent with the plain sense of the curses laid out in Deuteronomy.

(2) Likewise, many verses are quoted because they speak to the tremendous power of the divinity. Without directly adjuring or commanding God, such verses could be used to recall past acts

---

[26] AMB 9:7–9 (Naveh and Shaked 1987, 174–176).

of divine provision and protection in order to establish a precedent or paradigm for such actions in the present.[27] The bowl MS 2053/159 (Levene 2003, 100–102), for instance, quotes the Song of the Sea as part of an incantation written to anathematise, ban, and annul an evil lilith from appearing to the bowl owner in various frightening guises (including the form of the bowl owner's dead mother). It quotes three separate verses three times each, including Exod. 15.16:

תיפול עליהם אמתה ופחד בגדול זרועך ידמו כאבן עד יעבר עמך יהוה עד יעבר עם זו קנית

> Terror and dread fell upon them, through the might of Your arm they stayed still as stone, till Your people passed, O LORD, till Your people passed whom You have ransomed.

In its original context, sung following the destruction of the Egyptian army at the Sea of Reeds, this verse speaks to the terror and

---

[27] Polzer (1986, 105–6) has argued that such quotations may have functioned as a form of divine inducement or indirect coercion. In this respect, biblical quotations would certainly have had the advantage of being more distinctive than mere requests, insofar as they serve to render God an addressee or narratee to his own actions. Compare the mode of address adopted in the Greek and Roman texts detailed in Hickson (1993, 33–43) and Furley and Bremer (2001, 2–5, 50–63) as well as the preference for declaratives in Latin curse-tablets—such as *commendo, mando, demando, defigo, deligo, obligo, devoveo, trado*—which stake out a fine ground of divine address that is neither entreaty nor command. Gordon (2019, 113) notes that, by "playing upon the force of such declaratives, the [writers of these magical texts] created a situation in which the ball was as it were suddenly in the court of the divine addressee(s): they had to deal with the move as best they could."

dread that fell upon the chiefs of Edom, the leaders of Moab, and all the inhabitants of Canaan as God shepherded his people amidst various threats. In the context of the bowl, terror and dread are presumably to fall upon the lilith infesting the bowl owner's home: the demon is threatened with the might of the divine arm while the protective paradigm instantiated by the verse is extended to the bowl owner. Such quotations—drawing upon historical or typological precedent—reflect a belief in the enduring nature of God and his actions.

(3) Similarly, partial quotations could be used (as epithets) to invoke divine attributes. For instance, in a bowl text that opens "By your name I act," an evil spirit identified as the daughter of Balʿin is adjured using several divine epithets drawn from biblical verses, all of which emphasise the might and the warlike character of the divinity:

> בישמיה דיה יהוה א יה יהוה איש מלחמה יהוה שמו יהוה עיזוז וגיבור יהוה גיבור ומלחמה יהוה מלך יהוה מאלך יהוה ימלך לעולם ועד מומינה עלכי אנתי רוחא בישתא דמיתקריא בת בלעין ...
>
> By the name of Yah, YHWH, A, Yah "YHWH is a man of war, YHWH is his name" (Exod. 15.3). "YHWH strong and mighty, YHWH mighty in battle" (Ps. 24.8). "YHWH is king, YHWH reigns, YHWH shall reign for ever and ever" (Ps. 10.16, Ps. 93.1, Exod. 15.18). I adjure you, you, evil spirit who is called daughter of Balʿin ...[28]

In this particular example, the quotations selected by the bowl writers do not just appeal to the divinity's immutable and warlike character, they also incorporate the divine name seven times;

---

[28] JBA 9:11–12 (Shaked et al. 2013, 79–81).

they were presumably selected and combined in part to achieve this significant numerological value.

In some bowl texts, whole biblical verses are quoted as names of power, using either בשמיה ד or בשום.

(4) Furthermore, a relevant factor in the selection of some verses may have been not just their perceived relevance to the apotropaic, curative, or comminative themes of the bowl text. Quotations may also have been selected for their ability to establish—in perlocutionary terms—the piety of the bowl owners and their fidelity to God's commandments. Verses such as Num. 9.23, Exod. 14.31, and Deut. 6.4, for instance, speak to trust in the One God and faithfulness to his commands.[29] Insofar as these units of scripture emphasise piety, they may have been designed to stand as testimony to the bowl owner's trust in God and to establish a protective paradigm built upon this trust. Exemplary in this regard are those bowls which interweave individual words from Deut. 6.4 with Ps. 91.1. This formulation combines a central statement of faith with the opening words of a psalm renowned for its anti-demonic powers; the result is an incantatory statement of faith/divine protection.

---

[29] Bhayro (2020) has also argued that the frequent quotation of Num. 9.23 in the bowls worked—again in perlocutionary fashion—to cast the bowl writer as working in collaboration with God, just as the efforts described in Num. 9.23 were achieved עַל פִּי יְהוָה 'upon the mouth of God' and בְּיַד מֹשֶׁה 'by the hand of Moses' (or the hand of the bowl writer). This might also go some way to explaining the frequent combination in the bowl texts of Num. 9.23 and Zech. 3.2, whose divine rebuke of Satan commences וַיֹּאמֶר יְהוָה.

Further to these general remarks on the use of the Bible in the bowls, the following sections survey in more detail some common thematic deployments of scripture in the bowls. They also touch upon several further issues with respect to the phenomenon of quotation in the bowl texts.

2.2.1. Prophylactics and Apotropaics

As mentioned previously, most bowls were written in order to protect their owners from the threat of demons and various forms of injurious magic. In service of these goals, we frequently find biblical quotations used to ward off demons and/or to establish the fact of divine protection. The Priestly Blessing in Num. 6.24–26 appears in several bowls, for instance. The protective paradigm attributed to these verses is made explicit in Targum Pseudo-Jonathan, which glosses יְבָרֶכְךָ יְהוָה וְיִשְׁמְרֶךָ 'The LORD bless you and keep you' as follows (amplifications upon the Hebrew in italics):

יברכינך ייי בכל עיסקך ויטרינך מן לילי ומזייעי ובני טיהררי ובני צפרירי ומזיקי וטלני

The LORD bless you *in all your endeavors* and keep you *from liliths and from fear demons and midday demons and morning demons and destroyers and shadow demons.*[30]

By far the most commonly quoted verse in the published bowl texts is Zech. 3.2, the quotation of which clearly pivots upon the divine rebuke that centres the verse:

---

[30] Cf. *Sifre Num.* 40, which also speaks specifically to the protection afforded by this verse from the class of demons known as מזקין 'destroyers'. This class of demons is a common target of the bowl texts.

וַיֹּאמֶר יְהוָה אֶל הַשָּׂטָן יִגְעַר יְהוָה בְּךָ הַשָּׂטָן וְיִגְעַר יְהוָה בְּךָ

And the LORD said to the *satan* (accuser), 'The LORD rebuke you, O *satan*, may the LORD rebuke you …

To threaten is also a way of warding off potential threats, and a striking example of this use of scripture is the deployment of Exod. 15.7 in a bowl targeted at a specific lilith:

וברוב גאונך ת(רע)ץ קומך תשלח חרונך יכלמו כקש

In the greatness of Your majesty You overthrew those who rose against You. You sent forth Your fury. It consumed them like stubble.[31]

The verse is inscribed in a circle around the drawing of the lilith in question, and the material arrangement of the text appears to have been designed to symbolically threaten the lilith with the fury of God and with the fate of the chaff.

2.2.2. Curative Uses

An excellent example of the curative use of scripture in the bowls is the deployment of Gen. 30.22 midway through an incantation for fertility and success in child birth. The quotation marks the end of one spell formula and the beginning of another. As previously observed, biblical quotations in the bowl texts are generally located either at the beginning or (more often) at the end of the incantation, and the somewhat unusual deployment of Gen. 30.22 in the middle of this text speaks to the specificity of its use. The bowl requests healing, fertility, and "living and abiding children" for Mihranahid daughter of Aḥat, while the quoted verse

---

[31] AMB 13:2 (Naveh and Shaked 1987, 198)

recounts how God remembered Rachel, listened to her, and opened her womb:

ויזכר אלהים את רחל וישמע אליה אלהים ויפתח את רחמה ויזכר

And God remembered Rachel, and God listened to her, and He opened her womb. And He remembered.[32]

Rachel had been unable to conceive and Gen. 30.22 signals the divine resolution to remedy her barrenness. The quotation thus invokes God to fulfil a specific blessing from the Torah for the benefit of the bowl owner, while the repetition in this bowl of "And He remembered" after the end of the verse serves both as a reaffirmation and to make explicit the constitutive role of the quotation in the bowl's magic.

The use of this quotation in the bowl also raises questions about the meronymic use of scripture in the bowls, i.e., the use of individual verses to invoke larger conceptual referents. Were quotations of Ps. 91.1, for example, understood to function *pars pro toto* for the entirety of Ps. 91? The wider psalm is steeped in metaphors for God's protective care, and because Ps. 91.1 is the beginning of a textual unit that goes on to detail various forms of divine protection from demons in particular, what seems implicit in its use is an intentional connection between the 'words quoted in the bowl' and the contiguous psalm as a whole.[33] Likewise,

---

[32] MFL 10895 (Bhayro 2017, 4–5).
[33] Scholars working on different apotropaic objects have noted the frequent *pars pro toto* deployment of specific verses from Ps. 91 on these objects, e.g. Judge (1987, 341); Kraus (2007, 487); Sanzo (2014, 106–20); Zenger (2000, 626). For the *pars pro toto* deployment of (psalmic)

Deut. 6.4 may have been quoted in the bowls not as an independent scriptural unit, but as an incipit that referred *pars pro toto* to the *Shemʿa* (Deut. 6.4–9, Deut. 11.13–21, and Num. 15.37–41) or to the Bedtime *Shemʿa* (where only Deut. 6.4–9 is recited).

With respect to Gen. 30.22, the question is whether the bowl writer had only this verse in mind, or whether the quotation was designed to invoke an even broader matrilineal paradigm wherein pregnancy is consistently framed as an act of God through the lives of Sarah, Rebecca, and Rachel. An example of this paradigm in action is to be found in a recipe for fertility from the Cairo Genizah that explicitly links Gen. 30.22 with Gen. 21.1 (Sarah) and Gen. 25.21 (Rebecca).[34] The recipe allies Rachel with the other matriarchs, Sarah and Rebecca, and works to emphasise *in triplicate* that infertility is actionable by God. The use of Gen. 30.22 in our bowl to tap into this broader (and even more powerful) paradigm would have served to significantly reinforce the action of the bowl.

---

incipits in magical texts more generally, see Rebiger (2003, 265–281) and Sanzo (2014).

[34] T-S K 1.157, fol. 1:21–31 (Schäfer and Shaked 1994, 8:111 f.) On the specific application of Gen. 30.22 in the Genizah materials, see Salzer (2010, 33, 68) and the texts T-S K 1.157, fol. 1:8 and 1:27–28 as well as the damaged Genizah recipe book T-S K 1.143 (Naveh and Shaked 1993, Genizah 18: 12:4–5 [189–197]). Cf. the citations of Gen. 21.1 ("And the LORD visited Sarah as He had said, and the LORD did for Sarah as He had spoken") in the Genizah amulets T-S K 1.157, fol. 1:12 and 1:29 and recipe book T-S K 1.157, fol. 1:9. On the broader matrilineal paradigm, see Salzer (2010, 266–271).

The study of the Bible in the bowls is only taking its first steps. It remains an open question whether certain bowl writers quoted specific biblical verses in order to invoke a larger conceptual referent than the 'mere' words quoted in the bowl. The use of incipits within the bowl corpus, as well as other meronymic uses of scripture, merit further investigation.

2.2.3. For Popularity and Success

Though the bowls were largely used to protect against demons and to address illnesses and ailments caused by or personified as demons, other genres of magic also make an appearance across the material medium of the bowls. Only a few examples of bowls for popularity and success have been published thus far, though a number of unpublished examples are known. Amongst the published bowls, we find Prov. 3.4 quoted in a text designed to bring about favour and success (in court) for Mahdukh daughter of Ispendarmed:

ומצא חן ושכל טוב בעיני אלהים ואדם

> And may he find grace and good understanding in the eyes of God and man.[35]

Another bowl written for success in business—and designed specifically to bring a multitude of customers to the gate of Wartan son of Miryay—quotes several verses from Isa. 60. Two of these verses emphasise abundance and the accumulation of great wealth, while the third verse construes Wartan's many customers metaphorically in terms of a vast cloud of birds:

---

[35] MS 1927/2:5 (Shaked 2005, 25–26).

פיתחו שערייך תמיד יומם ולילה ולא יסגרו להביא אליך חיל גוים ומלכיהם
נהוגים שיפעת גמלים תכסיך בכרי מידין ועיפה כולם מישבא יבואו זהב
ולבונה ישאו ותהילות יהוה יבשרו מי אלה כעב תעופנה וכיונים אל
ארובותיהם

Open your gates continually; and they shall not be shut day or night, to bring to you the wealth of nations; and their kings are led (Isa. 60.11). The abundance of camels shall cover you, dromedaries of Midian and Ephah; all of them from Sheba shall come; gold and incense they shall bring, and the praises of the LORD they shall announce (Isa. 60.6). Who are these that as a cloud fly, and as doves to their windows? (Isa. 60.8)[36]

2.2.4. Aggressive Uses

As noted above, the material medium of the bowls was also used for the writing of aggressive spells targeted at named individuals. This form of interpersonal engagement is to be found most commonly in counter-charms designed to return curses, demons, and other forms of (demonised) malice to their senders (often with interest). It is also to be found in more forthright texts that do not couch their aggression in terms of reciprocity. A good example of the former category is a bowl text designed to return a *yaror* or jackal-spirit to its original sender, Šišin daughter of Asmandukh. In service of this goal, the bowl writer uses Deut. 6.19 to construe Šišin as an enemy to be driven out:

להדוף א(ית) כל איביך מיפנך כאשר דבר יהוה

---

[36] SD 34:13–14 (Levene and Bhayro, 2005/2006).

> That all your enemies may be driven out before you, as the LORD has spoken.³⁷

An example of outright aggression in the bowls is to be found in a text cited above, AMB 9, which seeks the (painful) death of Judah son of Nanay. In service of this goal, the bowl writer quotes Ps. 69.24, Ps. 69.26, Exod. 22.23, and Lev. 26.29 in addition to the curses in Deut. 28.22, Deut. 28.35, and Deut. 28.28, culminating in Deut. 29.19. One function of these biblical curses—in addition to supplementing the various Aramaic curses applied to Judah son of Nanay—may have been to sanction the act of cursing the victim as a legitimate practice. By drawing upon Deuteronomy, the bowl writer is able to mark out Judah as someone who has committed a severe offence against the LORD and drawn down the righteous anger of God. Using these quotations, the bowl writer is able to emphasise the legitimacy of their aggressive magical action.³⁸

All of the foregoing examples illustrate how different units of scripture were appropriated by the bowl writers on the basis of their themes and (narrative) contents and the perceived consonance of these themes and contents with the bowl owners' specific needs. In some instances, the quotations demonstrate how biblical verses could be separated out from their original contexts

---

³⁷ VA 2484:19 (Levene 2013, 22–24).

³⁸ See Salzer (2013, 628–631) for the similar application of Lev. 6.5, Lev. 6.6, and Lev. 9.24 in order to draw a connection between the sacrificial cult of the Jerusalem Temple and the sending of a fever. In this light, the fever is sanctioned and connotes "an activity demanded by divine authority" (629).

using more creative forms of logic. This primarily 'bite-size' approach to the Bible in the bowls suggests that the bowl writers conceived of scripture largely as a repository or repertory of separable units.[39] These individual units could be used to invoke the powers associated with the precedent or thematic paradigm of the events and/or actions and/or divine characteristics narrated or described in a given quotation.

3.0. The Orthography of the Quotations in the Context of Late Antique Bible Transmission

The scriptural quotations in the bowls reflect varying degrees of correspondence to—or independence from—the orthography known to us from the later, medieval Masoretic manuscripts. In most cases, the quotations are characterised by a degree of 'free' spelling—primarily phonetic or *plene* spelling—that may be attributed to the reproduction of scripture from aural memory.[40]

---

[39] This selective approach to scriptural material in the manufacturing of the bowls would naturally have been dictated by pragmatic factors as well, including the limitations of the artefact: the writing surface of a small bowl can only include so much text, and it was thus necessary to separate smaller units of scripture from their larger wholes for this reason too. It is also necessary to keep in mind the ways in which the diverse body of bowl writers may have encountered scripture, whether through common engagement in the context of the liturgy—which would have focused attention on portions of scripture as sources of apotropaic or exorcistic power—or through encounters with written scripture.

[40] Indeed, quotations that are virtually identical to their (Babylonian and Tiberian) Masoretic counterpart are uncommon. The designation 'free' is a shorthand designed to express the partial independence of the

This makes them a unique source of insight into the Biblical Hebrew pronunciation traditions at the time of their production (see the following section). That said, it is rare to find completely 'free' spellings in the bowls, such as quotations where vowel letters are used extensively and in all types of syllables,[41] or where the orthography is wholly devoid of any Hebrew spelling conventions.

With respect to the Masoretic traditions, the fact that there is an overwhelming correspondence between the consonantal text of the Babylonian Masoretic manuscripts and the Tiberian Leningrad Codex (Ofer 2013) makes it very likely that both of these consonantal texts go back to a largely uniform consonantal source at the end of the Second Temple period. This, in turn, implies that a consonantal text very similar to the Masoretic text would have been in existence also in 'Talmudic' Babylonia. Furthermore, there is evidence of the rabbis' attempts to standardise the biblical scrolls. The Babylonian Talmud, for example, prohibits the keeping of 'uncorrected scrolls.'[42] Almost certainly, this rabbinic censorship would have applied first and foremost to scrolls intended for public reading; scrolls in private ownership

---

quotations from the conservative Biblical Hebrew writing conventions that we know from the medieval Masoretic codices (cf. Golinets 2013 and the references therein) and which presumably also existed in the period of bowl production.

[41] For vowel letters in Hebrew and their history, see Andersen and Forbes (2013).

[42] For details, see Rosenthal (1982, 403).

or in very remote communities were likely sometimes characterised by a more independent orthography (Rosenthal 1982, 403, citing Liberman).

The existence of a 'free' biblical orthography within the quotations is thus highly significant. At the very least, it indicates that, for the bowl producers, the successful deployment of scriptural quotations in the bowl texts did not hinge on their full adherence to 'normative' (or 'proto-Masoretic') biblical orthography. This in turn likely means that—despite the rabbinic notion of written Torah and the likely pressure towards standardisation—scriptural authority for the Jews of late antique Babylonia did not automatically imply a textual-orthographic uniformity, at least in some social-religious domains. On a more pragmatic level, the variation in the orthography is almost certainly indicative of limited access to written texts of the Hebrew Bible, and perhaps especially 'proto-Masoretic' written texts of the Bible.

That said, the tendency to 'free' orthography in the quotations should not be taken as a sign of weakness or fragility in the Hebrew Bible transmission of late antique Babylonia. On the contrary, the quotations bear witness to the robustness and resourcefulness of both written and oral scripture transmission. Regarding the written component, as alluded to above, the bowls tend to preserve some general conventions of Hebrew orthography. A graphically salient tendency is the retention of ה (h) as the word-final vowel letter for the *a* and (in some cases) *e* vowels. This makes the Hebrew scriptural quotations visually distinct from their surrounding Aramaic text, in which א (ʾ) predominates in such word-final contexts. This, in turn, indicates that even though the bowl writers were probably often not quoting from a (standardised) written text, they had nevertheless been educated to read (and write) Biblical Hebrew.[43] This points to the centrality of the Bible in late antique Babylonian Jewish education.

On the other hand, the 'free' orthography of most quotations is likely indicative of quotation from aural memory. In other words, the bowl writer retained the biblical passage in question in memory, having heard it in public performance (cantillation) or having recited it in private prayer. Evidence for this in the quotations comes from the dozens of words whose orthography betrays a pausal form. Pausal forms are morphological alternatives available for some words when these words occur at the end of larger syntactic units such as clauses.[44] Together with features such as melodic contour and speed variation, pausal forms would have been part of stylised Hebrew performance, preserved by Jewish communities to-date. These features of the quotations, in turn, hint at the vitality of oral Bible performance and recitation, and at the (likely) prevalence of this practice within the Jewish community.[45]

An example of a pausal form is the verb תוכילו (*twkylw*) 'you (MP) will eat' (from Lev. 26.29 in bowl AMB 9:9; MT תֹּאכֵלוּ). In a regular, contextual form, the consonant כ (k) in the medieval

---

[43] See further Reif (2017).

[44] See further Fassberg (2013) and Jacobson (2013).

[45] Further to this, it is possible that—when quoting scripture—some bowl writers recalled many other forms as pausal from aural memory, but did not explicitly indicate them as pausal in the orthography due to conventional restrictions or a lack of obvious letters to use for that purpose.

Babylonian tradition would have been followed by a (vocalic) *shewa* (i.e. [a]). Thus, the vowel letter ׳ (*y*) is unexpected here for a contextual form.[46] A pausal form, on the other hand, would be vocalised in the Babylonian manuscripts with *ē*, the equivalent of the Tiberian *ṣere*. Since ׳ (*y*) is commonly used to represent *ē* in the quotations, it is likely that here as well it represents the vowel *ē* and thus a pausal reading, also attested in this verse in the MT (I Firkovitch B19A; Molin 2017, pp. 86–87).

4.0. Reconstructing the Language behind the Quotations

Used carefully, the tendency to 'free' spelling in the biblical quotations in the bowls can shed some light on the Hebrew pronunciation traditions behind the quotations. Like biblical text critics, however, scholars of the quotations in the bowls have to consider a variety of explanations for the orthographic features displayed in the bowls. Potential explanations for specific features range from scribal errors to textual variants in the (written or oral) *vorlage* of the bowl writers. Linguistic proposals must also be taken into consideration. Moreover, some features of the quotations reflect deliberate manipulations, such as the deliberate omission of the five final letters of the word משנאיך 'those who hate you (MS)' from the quotation of Num. 10.35 in AMB 3:5 (Naveh and Shaked

---

[46] To our knowledge, there are no cases of vowel letters (e.g., ׳ [*y*]) for the sound corresponding to the Masoretic vocalic *shewa* (realised as a short *a* in both the Tiberian and Babylonian tradition; cf. Khan 2013, par. 24; Molin 2017, 40). On the other hand, such use of ׳ is attested in the Aramaic of the spells (Juusola 1999, 44–45).

1987, 146). This omission was most probably designed to negate the threat of the bowl owner's enemies, who are construed through the quotation as the enemies of God. In addition, it is possible that a handful of unusual spellings in the scriptural material reflects a phenomenon known as orthoepy: a careful, highly performative pronunciation of Biblical Hebrew.[47] Since orthoepic features would likely have occurred in a limited, 'elite' form of Bible cantillation, possible instances of orthoepic features in the quotations should not be taken as evidence for their general prevalence in late antique Mesopotamia.

A final methodological point due here reflects the fact that the transcription of some of the quotations within the published bowl material likely reflects a scholarly bias in favour of Tiberian Hebrew and against the virtually unknown Babylonian tradition, especially in cases where the letters on the artefacts are not clear or ambiguous to begin with. This is illustrated by the form transcribed in this catalogue as יתלנון (*ytlnwn*) 'dwells (MS)' (from Ps. 91.1 in bowl VA 2423:23). This emends the original transcription יתלנין (*ytlnyn*) by Levene (2013). The grapheme י (*y*) chosen by Levene would have been a suitable vowel letter for *ē* (Tiberian *ṣere*). In the Tiberian tradition, this vowel is expected in the contextual (i.e., non-pausal) form of this verb, assuming that this verb belongs to the *hitpolel* conjugation (i.e. יִתְלֹנֵן). In the corresponding Babylonian contextual form, however, we find the

---

[47] For the concept of orthoepy and its apparent manifestations in the Tiberian tradition, see Khan (2020). For possible examples in the bowl texts, see Molin (2017, 18–19 and 49–50), where the quotation of Num. 10.35 is discussed.

vowel *a* (corresponding to the Tiberian *pataḥ*; Yeivin 1985, I:577),[48] which would certainly not have been represented using the letter י by the bowl writer. The expected vowel letter would be ו (*w*). This reading of יתלונ instead of יתלניִ is possible because the written forms of י and ו are indistinguishable in most bowl texts, including VA 2423. In this bowl, ו could have been chosen to represent the back *a* vowel, i.e. *å* (the sound corresponding to Tiberian *qameṣ*, IPA [ɔː]). *å* is expected in the pausal forms of the verb in question in both the Babylonian and Tiberian traditions (Molin 2017, 85–86). The use of ו for the equivalent of the vowel *qameṣ* is attested in at least a dozen cases in the biblical quotations in the bowls (Molin 2017, 23–27).

In general, the Hebrew behind the quotations is decisively Babylonian.[49] Indeed, some features explicitly conform to the medieval Babylonian pronunciation over the Tiberian one. This can be illustrated by the vocalisation of the conjunction ו (*w*) 'and'. Consider the form ויבמצוק (*wybmṣwq*) in the repeated, inverse quotation from Deut. 28.57 in the bowl JBA 46:11–12 (Shaked et al. 2013, 208–209). In Babylonian Bible manuscripts, when this conjunction (realised with different vowels depending on its phonetic environment) is followed by a consonant with another consonant immediately after it,[50] an epenthetic *i* is inserted after the

---

[48] In other words, only *hitpolal*—and not *hitpolel*—is used in the Babylonian tradition.

[49] For the phonology of Babylonian Hebrew, see Khan (2013).

[50] That is, when the first consonant after the conjunction is followed by a *shewa*, a phonological zero.

conjunction (Yeivin 1985, II:1152).[51] This is in line with the orthography ויב (*wyb*) 'and in' in the example in question. Here, י (*y*) is inserted between 'and' and 'in.' The sequence would thus have been pronounced *wib̲*, which is expected, since the preposition ב (*b*) is followed here by another consonant. This contrasts with the Tiberian tradition, where the same cluster would most likely be resolved as *wub̲*, the conjunction being pointed ו in such cases (Khan 2020, 176–181). Spellings such as ויב(מצוק) thus bear witness to the Babylonian type of cluster resolution, which distinguishes it from the Tiberian system (Molin 2017, 80–81; Frim 2021, 42–43). Other distinctly Babylonian features include the presence of distinct vowels ('vocalisation') in the vicinity of the gutturals (the pharyngeal and glottal consonants) in some environments. One also encounters the preservation of short *u*, *o*, *e*, and *i* in cases where the shortening causes a change in their quality in the Tiberian tradition.[52]

Finally, some orthographic features betray the interference of the bowl writers' vernacular: Jewish Babylonian Aramaic.[53] Perhaps the most salient of these contact influences is the spread of pharyngealisation ('emphasis spread' or 'suprasegmental pharyngealisation/emphasis'). In the corpus of the quotations, this spread is apparently induced by the pharyngealised ('emphatic')

---

[51] See also Boyarin (1978, 146) for a discussion of this feature in JBA.

[52] For a longer list of Babylonian features evidenced by the quotations, see Molin (2020) and Frim (2021).

[53] The influence of other contact languages (such as Mandaic) is also possible in principle, though the evidence for it in the quotations is much more speculative (cf. Molin 2017, 45 and 64 for possible cases).

phonemes צ (ṣ) and ט (ṭ), the uvular ק (q), as well as ר (r) and the pharyngeals ח (ḥ) and ע (ʿ). From these phonemes, pharyngealisation is extended to other phonemes in their vicinity.⁵⁴ Cases of secondary pharyngealisation induced by the emphatics and q are attested in the Hebrew of the Babylonian Talmud (Breuer 2002, 113–116) and in Jewish Babylonian Aramaic sources (Bar-Asher Siegal 2013, 71–72). The tell-tale signs of such secondary pharyngealisation in the biblical quotations in the bowls are orthographic changes from the non-emphatic alveolars ד (d) and ת (t) to ט (ṭ), their emphatic counterpart, as well as from ש/ס (both s) to the emphatic צ (ṣ).⁵⁵ Examples include מקטש (mqṭš) instead of מקדש (mqdš) 'temple' in the quotation of Exod. 15.15 in the bowl IM 141803 (Faraj 2010, 206–207), where the change of ד to ט is induced by the uvular ק, and המעט (hmʿṭ) instead of המעד (hmʿd) 'make stand (MS IMP)' in the quotation of Ps. 69.24 in AMB 9 (Naveh and Shaked 1987, 174–176).

As the foregoing discussion shows, the JBA bowl texts are valuable early sources of information for the Babylonian Hebrew vocalisation tradition. It is hoped that the present catalogue will facilitate further research in both this and other respects.

---

⁵⁴ q and r are attested as inducing pharyngealisation (in their environment or in the phoneme itself for r) in some languages, including North-Eastern Neo-Aramaic. For an overview of pharyngealisation, see Molin (2021, 65–66) and the references therein.

⁵⁵ For parallels in the Aramaic of the bowls, see Ford (2012).

5.0. Note on the Transcription of Bowl Texts

I have sought in every case to check the quotations reproduced in the catalogue against photographs of the bowl texts. As such, the readings of some quotations in the catalogue differ from those provided by the original editors of certain bowls. In some instances, however, verification of the published text of the bowl has not proven possible. The bowl IM 9736, for example, was published by Gordon (1941, 349–350) without any photographs, while the present whereabouts of this bowl are unknown (Saar 2013), making it impossible to secure photographs of the text. In other cases, the photographs accompanying editions of published bowls are of insufficient quality to confirm the accurate reading of the text and it has not always proven practicable to secure new photographs of these bowls.

In any and every case, however, users of the catalogue should compare the readings in the catalogue with the published edition of the text and—where possible—with high-resolution photographs of the bowl, as different scholars will reach different determinations with respect to uncertain or partially preserved letters.

CATALOGUE OF BIBLICAL QUOTATIONS IN PUBLISHED JEWISH BABYLONIAN ARAMAIC MAGIC BOWLS

1.0. Note on the Catalogue

The quotation of individual verses is the most common form of quotation in the bowls, and the individual verse thus forms the basic unit of the catalogue. The following abbreviations and symbols are designed to indicate 'divergences' from this 'standard' (such as partial quotations, quotations of continuous verses, paraphrases, or conflations) and to help the user locate other features of interest (such as the addition of *targumim*). Where a *targum* accompanies the Hebrew, this is included in the relevant entry. Likewise, the catalogue reproduces all repetitions, self-corrections, and magical inversions and omissions of (parts of) quotations. In the case of certain partial quotations, their brevity means that it is not possible to determine which of two biblical passages is being quoted. In these cases, the equals symbol (=) is used to indicate the other verses that may represent the source of the quotation. In such cases, as well as cases of conflation and the interweaving of separate verses, the bowl appears twice in the catalogue. For example, where alternating words from Deut. 6.4 and Ps. 91.1 are written one after the other, the text of the bowl appears under both Deut. 6.4 and Ps. 91.1 in the catalogue.

Finally, *targumim* in the MT/TARGUM column have been vocalised according to the Babylonian reading tradition presented in Sperber (2004), though these entries have been 'Tiberianised' for readers unfamiliar with the supra-linear system of markings.

2.0. Abbreviations and Symbols

Abbreviations and Symbols (Left-Hand Column)

א	indicates biblical passages that are not extant amongst the finds from the Judaean Desert[1]
S	indicates a bowl text that consists solely of scriptural quotations
T	indicates that the Hebrew quotation is accompanied by a **Targum**
𝓣	indicates the appearance of a Targum alone
∮	indicates the quotation of two or more continuous verses
P	indicates the **partial** quotation of an individual verse
E	indicates the deployment of a (partial) quotation as (part of) a divine **epithet**
C	indicates the **conflation** of two or more verses, cf. I(nterweaving)
I	indicates the **interweaving** of alternating words from different verses

---

[1] Where only small portions of a biblical verse are preserved in the Hebrew finds from the Judean Desert, or where the verse is preserved only in translation, I also mark the pertinent verse in the catalogue with the א symbol. For instance, only a handful of letters from the Hebrew of Zech. 3.2 is preserved in 4QXIIe (4Q80); and while 8ḤevXIIgr preserves the verse in Greek, the quotations of this verse in the bowl texts are the oldest surviving complete witnesses to Zech. 3.2 in Hebrew.

⇄   indicates the other verse(s) included in a conflation or interweaving

≅   indicates a paraphrase

=   indicates the potential location of partial quotations (rarely: conflations) whose biblical referent cannot be determined with certainty

Further to the above, I employ several abbreviations and symbols in the COMMENTS column of the catalogue. I use these to indicate the use of explicit citation formulae and the appearance of 'clusters' of biblical quotations at common points in the bowl texts (e.g. at the end of the text, and less frequently at the beginning). In the case of such clusters, I note all of the clustered verses in the order in which they appear. I also use this column to indicate any other biblical verses that appear in the same bowl. Finally, where the stated or apparent purpose of the bowl is not to ward off, trap, or otherwise neutralise demons and the like, I use this column to note the purpose of the bowl in question, for example, to achieve fertility or success in love or business, to curse, etc.

Abbreviations and Symbols (Comments Column)

❖   indicates a **cluster** of biblical verses

CF   indicates the use of a **citation formula**

EC   indicates an **epithet cluster**, where a divine epithet is built by stringing (partial) verses together

3.0. Sigla

Sigla Used in the Transcription of Quotations

[ ]	restored letters
{ }	superfluous letters
< >	scribal omission, used only of whole words
אבגד	partially preserved letters whose reading can nevertheless be determined
( )	uncertain letters
[...]	Text missing due to the loss of fragments from damaged bowls or the extensive effacement of the bowl surface

4.0. Reference Guide to Bowl Texts

Abbreviations and Reference Guide to Major Publications of Bowl Texts

AIT	Montgomery, *Aramaic Incantation Texts* (1913)
AMB	Naveh and Shaked, *Amulets and Magic Bowls* (1985)
CAMIB	Segal, *Catalogue of the Aramaic Bowls in the British Museum* (2000)
Corpus	Levene, *Corpus of Magic Bowls* (2003)
Curses	Levene, *Jewish Aramaic Curse Texts* (2013)
Isbell	Isbell, *Corpus of the Aramaic Incantation Bowls* (1975)
JBA	Shaked, Ford and Bhayro, *Aramaic Bowl Spells*, vol. 1 (2013) = JBA 1–64

	Shaked, Ford and Bhayro, *Aramaic Bowl Spells*, vol. 2 (2022) = JBA 65–119
MSF	Naveh and Shaked, *Magic Spells and Formulae* (1993)
SHM	Fain, Ford, and Lyavdansky, "Aramaic Incantation Bowls at the State Hermitage Museum" (2016)
ZHS	Müller-Kessler, *Zauberschalentexte in der Hilprecht-Sammlung* (2005)

Where JBA bowl texts have been published in one of the foregoing publications, I refer to them using the abbreviations above and their sequence or page number, e.g., JBA 64, Isbell 21, or Curses: 22–24.

Where JBA bowl texts have been published in individual editions, I refer to them using author name and year of publication, e.g., Bhayro 2017.

Where several JBA bowl texts appear in one publication, I refer to them using author name, year of publication, and page number, e.g., Gordon 1984: 238.

5.0. Catalogue of Biblical Quotations

QUOTATION	MT/TARGUM	BOWL	PUBLICATION	COMMENTS
ט Gen. 27.28 ⇄ Isa. 60.11 כ מזונה והוית ≈ דראתו עיני {עינך} הפתח שער ומפ[ר]	Gen. 27.28 (Tg. Onq.) וְיִתֶּן לָךְ יְיָ מִטַּלָּא דִשְׁמַיָּא וּמִטּוּבָא דְאַרְעָא וְסוּגְעֵי עֲבוּר וַחֲמָר׃	MS 1911/1	JBA 65	'For (the) livelihood' (למזוני) of the beneficiary ❖ Isa. 60.11 ↔ Gen. 27.28 Other quotations: ❖ Exod. 3.15, Isa. 40.31 CF: שובר
ט Gen. 27.28 ⇄ Isa. 60.11 כ מזונה [דלא] והוית ≈ דראתו עיני מנך הפתח יממ	Gen. 27.28 (Tg. Onq.) וְיִתֶּן לָךְ יְיָ מִטַּלָּא דִשְׁמַיָּא וּמִטּוּבָא דְאַרְעָא וְסוּגְעֵי עֲבוּר וַחֲמָר׃	MS 2053/56	JBA 67	❖ Isa. 60.11 ↔ Gen. 27.28 Other quotations: ❖ Exod. 3.15, Isa. 40.31; ❖ Ps. 121.7-8, Zech. 3.2 CF: שובר

	QUOTATION	MT/TARGUM	BOWL	PUBLICATION	COMMENTS
מ ק ש	Gen. 27.28 ⇄ Isa. 60.11 מיטרא ד[ירייא] אלהים דארעא ומ[נ]חו עמך יהב	Gen. 27.28 (Tg. Onq.) וְיִתֶּן לָךְ יְיָ מִטַּלָּא דִשְׁמַיָּא וּמִטּוּבָא דְאַרְעָא וְסַגְיוּת	MS 2053/69	JBA 95	✣ Isa. 60.11 ↔ Gen. 27.28 Other quotations: ✣ Exod. 3.15, Isa. 40.31 CF: שנאבר
מ ק ש	Gen. 27.28 ⇄ Isa. 60.11 מיטרא דשרייא אלהים דארעא וסגיאו עיבורא יהב	Gen. 27.28 (Tg. Onq.) וְיִתֶּן לָךְ יְיָ מִטַּלָּא דִשְׁמַיָּא וּמִטּוּבָא דְאַרְעָא וְסַגְיוּת	MS 2053/140	JBA 98	✣ Isa. 60.11 ↔ Gen. 27.28 Other quotations: ✣ Exod. 3.15, Isa. 40.31 CF: שנאבר
מ ק ש	Gen. 27.28 ⇄ Isa. 60.11 מארעא בד[טמא א]קר[י ...] [יהב] עמכן יבהל מנהם	Gen. 27.28 (Tg. Onq.) וְיִתֶּן לָךְ יְיָ מִטַּלָּא דִשְׁמַיָּא וּמִטּוּבָא דְאַרְעָא וְסַגְיוּת	MS 2053/215	JBA 101	✣ Isa. 60.11 ↔ Gen. 27.28 Other quotations: ✣ Exod. 3.15, Isa. 40.31 CF: שנאבר

QUOTATION	MT/TARGUM	BOWL	PUBLICATION	COMMENTS
Gen. 30.22 ויזכר אלהים את רחל וישמע אליה אלהים ויפתח את רחמה	Gen. 30.22 וַיִּזְכֹּר אֱלֹהִים אֶת רָחֵל וַיִּשְׁמַע אֵלֶיהָ אֱלֹהִים וַיִּפְתַּח אֶת רַחְמָהּ	MFL 10895	Bhayro 2017	For fertility and success in childbirth Other quotations: Zech. 3.2
Gen. 49.18 לישועתך קויתי יהוה	Gen. 49.18 לִישׁוּעָתְךָ קִוִּיתִי יְהוָה	MS 2053/47	JBA 87	
Gen. 49.22 בן פרת יוסף בן פרת עלי עין בנות צעדה עלי שור	Gen. 49.22 בֵּן פֹּרָת יוֹסֵף בֵּן פֹּרָת עֲלֵי עָיִן בָּנוֹת צָעֲדָה עֲלֵי שׁוּר	M 5	Shaked 1999: 194	Written on the exterior of the bowl
Gen. 49.22 [ב]ן פרת יוסף בן פרת [עלי] ע[ין] בנ[ות]	Gen. 49.22 בֵּן פֹּרָת יוֹסֵף בֵּן פֹּרָת עֲלֵי עָיִן בָּנוֹת צָעֲדָה עֲלֵי שׁוּר	BM 117869 BM 117870 BM 117871	CAMIB 71 + CAMIB 72 + CAMIB 73	Only several fragments of the bowl are preserved Other quotations: Isa. 40.12

	QUOTATION	MT/TARGUM	BOWL	PUBLICATION	COMMENTS
ת	Exod. 3.5	Exod. 3.5 (Tg. Onq.)	M 123	Corpus: 83-84, 89-90	CF: כמה דאמר ליה למשה באסנא, 'The same (name) he told Moses at the burning bush.'
E	שַׁל נְעָלֶיךָ מֵעַל רַגְלֶיךָ	שְׁלַף סֵינָךְ מֵעַל רַגְלָךְ			
P		אֲרֵי אַתְרָא דְּאַתְּ קָאֵים עֲלוֹהִי אֲתַר קַדִּישׁ הוּא			
ת	Exod. 3.5	Exod. 3.5 (Tg. Onq.)	M 138	Corpus: 89-90	CF: כמה דאמר ליה למשה באסנא, 'The same (name) he told Moses at the burning bush.'
E	שַׁל נְעָלֶיךָ מֵעַל	שְׁלַף סֵינָךְ מֵעַל רַגְלָךְ			
P		אֲרֵי אַתְרָא דְּאַתְּ קָאֵים עֲלוֹהִי אֲתַר קַדִּישׁ הוּא			
ת	Exod. 3.5	Exod. 3.5 (Tg. Onq.)	MS 2053/216	Corpus: 89-90	CF: כמה דאמר ליה למשה באסנא, 'The same (name) he told Moses at the burning bush.'
E	שַׁל נְעָלֶיךָ מֵעַל רַגְלֶיךָ	שְׁלַף סֵינָךְ מֵעַל רַגְלָךְ			
P		אֲרֵי אַתְרָא דְּאַתְּ קָאֵים עֲלוֹהִי אֲתַר קַדִּישׁ הוּא			

	QUOTATION	MT/TARGUM	BOWL	PUBLICATION	COMMENTS
E	Exod. 3.15	Exod. 3.15	MS 1911/1	JBA 65	'For (the) livelihood' (למזוני) of the beneficiary
P	זה שמי לעלם וזה זכרו	ויאמר עוד אלהים אל משה כה תאמר אל בני ישראל יהוה אלהי אבתיכם אלהי אברהם אלהי יצחק ואלהי יעקב שלחני אליכם זה שמי לעלם וזה זכרי לדר דר			Other quotations: ❖ Exod. 3.15, Isa. 40.31 ❖ Isa. 60.11 ↔ Gen. 27.28
E	Exod. 3.15	Exod. 3.15	MS 2053/56	JBA 67	
P	זה [זה] שמי לעלם וזה [זכרו]	ויאמר עוד אלהים אל משה כה תאמר אל בני ישראל יהוה אלהי אבתיכם אלהי אברהם אלהי יצחק ואלהי יעקב שלחני אליכם זה שמי לעלם וזה זכרי לדר דר			❖ Exod. 3.15, Isa. 40.31 Other quotations: ❖ Isa. 60.11 ↔ Gen. 27.28; ❖ Ps. 121.7-8, Zech. 3.2

QUOTATION	MT/TARGUM	BOWL	PUBLICATION	COMMENTS
E Exod. 3.15	Exod. 3.15	MS 2053/69	JBA 95	❖ Exod. 3.15, Isa. 40.31
P זה שמי לעל[ם] זה זכרי לד[ר] דר	כֹּה תֹאמַר אֶל בְּנֵי יִשְׂרָאֵל יְהוָה אֱלֹהֵי אֲבֹתֵיכֶם אֱלֹהֵי אַבְרָהָם אֱלֹהֵי יִצְחָק וֵאלֹהֵי יַעֲקֹב שְׁלָחַנִי אֲלֵיכֶם זֶה שְּׁמִי לְעֹלָם וְזֶה זִכְרִי לְדֹר דֹּר			Other quotations: ❖ Isa. 60.11 ↔ Gen. 27.28
E Exod. 3.15	Exod. 3.15	MS 2053/140	JBA 98	❖ Exod. 3.15, Isa. 40.31
P זה זכרי לדלעלם זה שמי לד[ר] דר	כֹּה תֹאמַר אֶל בְּנֵי יִשְׂרָאֵל יְהוָה אֱלֹהֵי אֲבֹתֵיכֶם אֱלֹהֵי אַבְרָהָם אֱלֹהֵי יִצְחָק וֵאלֹהֵי יַעֲקֹב שְׁלָחַנִי אֲלֵיכֶם זֶה שְּׁמִי לְעֹלָם וְזֶה זִכְרִי לְדֹר דֹּר			Other quotations: ❖ Isa. 60.11 ↔ Gen. 27.28

	QUOTATION	MT/TARGUM	BOWL	PUBLICATION	COMMENTS
E	Exod. 3.15	Exod. 3.15	MS 2053/215	JBA 101	❖ Exod. 3.15, Isa. 40.31
P	[זה] שמי לעלם זה זכרי לד׳׳ר	כה תאמר אל בני ישראל יהוה אלהי אבתיכם אלהי אברהם אלהי יצחק ואלהי יעקב שלחני אליכם זה שמי לעלם וזה זכרי לדר דר			Other quotations: ❖ Isa. 60.11 ↔ Gen. 27.28 The writing is extremely faded
E	Exod. 3.15	Exod. 3.15	MS 1927/9	Shaked 2005: 27	❖ Exod. 3.15, Num. 6.24-26
P	זה זכרי שמי לעלם [....] דר דר	כה תאמר אל בני ישראל יהוה אלהי אבתיכם אלהי אברהם אלהי יצחק ואלהי יעקב שלחני אליכם זה שמי לעלם וזה זכרי לדר דר			The text of the bowl is heavily effaced

QUOTATION	MT/TARGUM	BOWL	PUBLICATION	COMMENTS
Exod. 3.15	Exod. 3.15	MS 1927/43	JBA 15	Paraphrase deployed as an invocation
האבה׳ האבהם מצב אחר קנט׳ ישר[עו] [הז]ב [—] אשם הזב [הק]בר שם אלה׳ הזב דר דר׳[י]	לה תאמר אל בני ישראל יהוה אלהי אבתיכם אלהי אברהם אלהי יצחק ואלהי יעקב שלחני אליכם זה שמי לעלם וזה זכרי לדר דר			
Exod. 3.15	Exod. 3.15	MS 2053/212	JBA 60	Paraphrase deployed as an invocation The writing is extremely faded
באברהן ירבק {האבה} [א]ברהם [ה]זב ורב יצחק — הזב שם לעלם דר דר	לה תאמר אל בני ישראל יהוה אלהי אבתיכם אלהי אברהם אלהי יצחק ואלהי יעקב שלחני אליכם זה שמי לעלם וזה זכרי לדר דר			

	QUOTATION	MT/TARGUM	BOWL	PUBLICATION	COMMENTS
E ≈	Exod. 3.15	Exod. 3.15 אמרן מהרא מגב אמרן אהיה אשר אהיה יהיה שמע ישראל יהוה אלהינו יהוה אחד הדין (xx) דבריה	CBS 9013 אלהי אברהם אלהי יצחק ואלהי יעקב אלהא דאברהם אלהא דיצחק ואלהא דיעקב שלח רפא ומסי לידי	AIT 8[57]	Paraphrase deployed as an invocation
P ≈	Exod. 14.20	Exod. 14.20 אתא בין משרית דישראל ובין משרית מצראי והוה עננא וחשוכא למצראי ולישראל נהיר כוליה ליליא ולא קרב דין לות דין כל ליליה	IM 9736 ויבא בין מחנה מצרים ובין מחנה ישראל ויהי הענן והחשך ויאר את הלילה ולא קרב זה אל זה	Saar 2013[58]	For separating or sowing discord between a man and a woman

---

[57] Cf. Montgomery (1913, 160) who sees a conflation of Isa. 49.24 and Isa. 30.29 (and presumably Exod. 3.15).
[58] Exod. 14.20 appears to conclude the incantation, though the second half of the verse is missing from the original transcription of the bowl in Gordon (1941, 349–350). Gordon states that the bowl contains 12 lines of text, but he reproduces only 10, and it is unclear whether these two lost lines are missing from the opening or the closing of the

QUOTATION	MT/TARGUM	BOWL	PUBLICATION	COMMENTS
ℵ Exod. 14.31	Exod. 14.31 וַיַּרְא יִשְׂרָאֵל אֶת־הַיָּד הַגְּדֹלָה אֲשֶׁר עָשָׂה יְהוָה בְּמִצְרַיִם וַיִּירְאוּ הָעָם אֶת־יְהוָה וַיַּאֲמִינוּ בַּיהוָה וּבְמֹשֶׁה עַבְדּוֹ	JNF 124 וירא ישראל את היד [הגד]לה אשר עשה יהוה במצרים [וי]יראו העם את יהוה	Ford 2016: 153-154	✣ Deut. 6.4, Ps. 91.1, Exod. 14.31
ℵ Exod. 14.31	Exod. 14.31 וַיַּרְא יִשְׂרָאֵל אֶת־הַיָּד הַגְּדֹלָה אֲשֶׁר עָשָׂה יְהוָה בְּמִצְרַיִם וַיִּירְאוּ הָעָם אֶת־יְהוָה וַיַּאֲמִינוּ בַּיהוָה וּבְמֹשֶׁה עַבְדּוֹ	MS 1927/50 וירא ישראל את היד הגדלה אשר עשה יהוה במצרים וייראו העם את יהוה ויאמינו ביהוה ובמשה עבדו	JBA 116	CF: כתב בתה Other quotations: Ps. 114.3 (T), Isa. 6.3

bowl. Gordon did not provide a photograph of the bowl with his edition, nor have subsequent attempts to locate the bowl in the Iraq Museum proven successful (Saar 2013). The opening of the incantation conforms with other introductory formulae, however. As such—if the text of this bowl does indeed comprise 12 lines—then the two lines missing from Gordon's transcription may have included Exod. 14.20b.

	QUOTATION	MT/TARGUM	BOWL	PUBLICATION	COMMENTS
א E	Exod. 15.3 יְהוָה אִישׁ מִלְחָמָה יְהוָה שְׁמוֹ	Exod. 15.3 יְהוָה אִישׁ מִלְחָמָה יְהוָה שְׁמוֹ	MS 1927/8	JBA 1	**EC:** Exod. 15.3, Ps. 24.8, Ps. 10.16 ↔ Ps. 93.1 ↔ Exod. 15.18 Invoked as name of power: בשמיה ד Other Quotations: Ps. 104.20
א E	Exod. 15.3 יְהוָה אִישׁ מִלְחָמָה יְהוָה שְׁמוֹ	Exod. 15.3 יְהוָה אִישׁ מִלְחָמָה יְהוָה שְׁמוֹ	MS 1927/45	JBA 3	See above
א E P	Exod. 15.3 יְהוָה שְׁמוֹ	Exod. 15.3 יְהוָה אִישׁ מִלְחָמָה יְהוָה שְׁמוֹ	MS 1927/47	JBA 4	See above The bowl writer (accidentally) omitted the first half of the verse.

Catalogue 57

	QUOTATION	MT/TARGUM	BOWL	PUBLICATION	COMMENTS
M	Exod. 15.3	Exod. 15.3	MS 1927/64	JBA 5	See above
E	יהוה איש מלחמה יהוה שמו	יְהוָה אִישׁ מִלְחָמָה יְהוָה שְׁמוֹ			Other Quotations: Ps. 104.20, Zech. 3.2
M	Exod. 15.3	Exod. 15.3	MS 2053/10	JBA 6	See above
E	יהוה א[יש מלח]מה ה יהוה שמה	יְהוָה אִישׁ מִלְחָמָה יְהוָה שְׁמוֹ			Cartouche
M	Exod. 15.3	Exod. 15.3	MS 2053/12	JBA 7	See above
E	יהוה איש מלחמה יהוה שמו	יְהוָה אִישׁ מִלְחָמָה יְהוָה שְׁמוֹ			Cartouche
M	Exod. 15.3	Exod. 15.3	MS 2053/183	JBA 9	See above
E	יהוה איש מלחמה יהוה שמו	יְהוָה אִישׁ מִלְחָמָה יְהוָה שְׁמוֹ			
M	Exod. 15.3	Exod. 15.3	MS 2053/185	JBA 10	See above
E	יהוה איש מלחמה [יהוה שמו]	יְהוָה אִישׁ מִלְחָמָה יְהוָה שְׁמוֹ			Cartouche

	QUOTATION	MT/TARGUM	BOWL	PUBLICATION	COMMENTS
א	Exod. 15.3	Exod. 15.3	LO.831	Bhayro 2014	See above
E	יהוה איש מלחמה יהוה שמו יהוה שמו יהוה איש מלחמה	יְהוָה אִישׁ מִלְחָמָה יְהוָה שְׁמוֹ			
א	Exod. 15.3	Exod. 15.3	M 156	Corpus: 115-116	See above
E	יהוה איש מלחמה יהוה שמו	יְהוָה אִישׁ מִלְחָמָה יְהוָה שְׁמוֹ			
א	Exod. 15.3	Exod. 15.3	MS 1927/29	JBA 2	See above
E	יהוה א[י]ש מלחמה יהוה שמו	יְהוָה אִישׁ מִלְחָמָה יְהוָה שְׁמוֹ			EC: Exod. 15.3, ——— The text of the bowl is heavily effaced
א	Exod. 15.3	Exod. 15.3	MS 2053/79	JBA 11	EC: Ps. 24.8, Exod. 15.3, Ps. 10.16 ↔ Ps. 93.1 ↔ Exod. 15.18
E	יהו[ה] איש מלחמה יהוה שמו	יְהוָה אִישׁ מִלְחָמָה יְהוָה שְׁמוֹ			Invoked as name of power: משמיה ד

Catalogue 59

	QUOTATION	MT/TARGUM	BOWL	PUBLICATION	COMMENTS
א E	Exod. 15.3 יהוה איש מלחמה יהוה שמו	Exod. 15.3 יְהֹוָה אִישׁ מִלְחָמָה יְהֹוָה שְׁמוֹ	MS 2053/178	JBA 12	See above
א	Exod. 15.7 הרוב גאונך תהרוס ק(מי)ך תקומ קמיך תשלח חרונך יאכלמו כקש	Exod. 15.7 וּבְרֹב גְּאוֹנְךָ תַּהֲרֹס קָמֶיךָ תְּשַׁלַּח חֲרֹנְךָ יֹאכְלֵמוֹ כַּקַּשׁ	VK 2	AMB 13	
φ S T	Exo.d 15.9-12 אמר איבא ארדף ואשיג אחלק שלל תמלאמו נפשי אריק חרבי תורישמו ידי [נ]שפת ברוחך כסמו ים צללו כעפרת במים אדירים מי כמכה באלם יהוה מי כמכה נאדר בקדש נורא תהלת עשה פלא [נטית]ה ימינך תבלעמו ארץ	Exod. 15.9-12 אָמַר אוֹיֵב אֶרְדֹּף אַשִּׂיג אֲחַלֵּק שָׁלָל תִּמְלָאֵמוֹ נַפְשִׁי אָרִיק חַרְבִּי תּוֹרִישֵׁמוֹ יָדִי (MT) אֲמַר סָנְאָה אֶרְדּוֹף אַדְבֵּיק אֲפַלֵּג בִּזְתָא תִּשְׂבַּע מִנְּהוֹן נַפְשִׁי אֲשְׁלוֹף חַרְבִּי תְּשֵׁיצֵינוּן יְדִי (Tg. Onq.) נָשַׁפְתָּ בְרוּחֲךָ כִּסָּמוֹ יָם צָלֲלוּ כַּעוֹפֶרֶת בְּמַיִם אַדִּירִים מִי כָמֹכָה בָּאֵלִם יְהוָה מִי כָּמֹכָה נֶאְדָּר בַּקֹּדֶשׁ נוֹרָא תְהִלֹּת עֹשֵׂה פֶלֶא נָטִיתָ יְמִינְךָ תִּבְלָעֵמוֹ אָרֶץ (MT)	HS 3030	Ford/Morgenstern 2020: 92-93	Interlinear targum

QUOTATION	MT/TARGUM	BOWL	PUBLICATION	COMMENTS
אמת חתומה בחתם אמת עליהן ברוך אתה יהוה אל(א)הנא דאברהם אבונן דגנבי [גנב] ביה יהוה יהוה ית נחש הקדמוני דאטעי חוה ית אדם אדם את חוה חוה את הבל הבל את קין קין את אחיו הוא אל{ה}א חד בלא זוגא ומלתא חדא בלא זוגא יהוה אל{ה}א חד (MT) יהוה אלהא הוא אלהא ומלתיה אמת (Tg. Onq.) נטית ימינך תבלעמו ארץ (MT) ארכינתא ימינך ובלעתנון ארעא (Tg. Onq.)				
T Exod. 15.12	Exod. 15.12 נטית ימינך תבלעמו ארץ (MT) ארכינתא ימינך ובלעתנון ארעא (Tg. Onq.)	IM 56544	ZHS 2a	✢ Isa. 50.11, Exod. 15.12 An allusive bowl text, whose various citations are invoked as names of power: בשמ

QUOTATION	MT/TARGUM	BOWL	PUBLICATION	COMMENTS
Exod. 15.14-17	Exod. 15.14-17	IM 141803	Faraj 2010: 206-207	❖ Exod. 15.14-17 [Exod. 15.14 x2], Zech. 3.2, Prov. 30.17
שמעו עמים ירגזון [I: 5-7] חיל אחז ישבי פלשת [IV: 6-7] אז נבהלו אלופי אדום אילי מואב יאחזמו רעד נמגו כל ישבי כנען [I: 1-4] [ע]תפל עליהם אימתה ופחד [גב]יל בגדל זרועך ידמו כאבן עד יעבר עמך יהוה עד יעבר עמ[ך(א)] זו קנית תבאמו ותטעמו בהר נחלתך מכון לשבתך פעלת יהוה מקדש אדני כוננו ידיך יהוה (הוה)ימלך לעלם ועד [FIGURE] יהוה איש מלחמה	Exod. 15.14-17		The text of the bowl is divided into four sections around a drawing of a demon. The text of Exod. 15.14 is repeated within the body of the demon.

QUOTATION	MT/TARGUM	BOWL	PUBLICATION	COMMENTS
Exod. 15.16 [ח׳]בא עליהם אימתא תפול יהוה עד די יעבור עם זו קנית עד דיעבור עמא דנן אדמתא תהוה אדוק באבניא רברביא ותהי [יהוה] קדם יי עמך עד דיעבור עמך דנן [יהוה יהוה] עד די יעבור עמא <דנאה> דכנא דנא קנית עד די יעבור עם יי קנית	Exod. 15.16 תִּפֹּל עֲלֵיהֶם אֵימָתָה וָפַחַד בִּגְדֹל זְרוֹעֲךָ יִדְּמוּ כָּאָבֶן עַד־יַעֲבֹר עַמְּךָ יְהוָה עַד־יַעֲבֹר עַם־זוּ קָנִיתָ	MS 2053/159	Corpus: 100-102	✧ Isa. 6.3 (3x), Exod. 15.16 (3x), Exod. 15.18 (3x)
Exod. 15.18 [יהו]ה י[מלך] [לעלם] ועד יהוה י[מלוך] לעלמי עלמיא יהוה ימלוך לעלם ועד	Exod. 15.18 יְהוָה יִמְלֹךְ לְעֹלָם וָעֶד	MS 2053/159	Corpus: 100-102	✧ Isa. 6.3 (3x), Exod. 15.16 (3x), Exod. 15.18 (3x)
Exod. 15.18 [יהו]ה ימלוך לעלם ועד	Exod. 15.18 יְהוָה יִמְלֹךְ לְעֹלָם וָעֶד	BM 91778	CAMIB 65	The bowl is fragmented

QUOTATION	MT/TARGUM	BOWL	PUBLICATION	COMMENTS
C Exod. 15.18 ⇄ Ps. 10.16 E ⇄ Ps. 93.1 P	SEE Ps. 10.16 BELOW [12 ENTRIES]			
Exod. 22.23	Exod. 22.23 וְחָרָה אַפִּי וְהָרַגְתִּי אֶתְכֶם בֶּחָרֶב וְהָיוּ נְשֵׁיכֶם אַלְמָנוֹת וּבְנֵיכֶם יְתֹמִים יְתֹמִ[ים]	—	AMB 9	For cursing a named individual **CF:** קמהי עליה קאה דמהן Other quotations: ✥ Ps. 69.24, Ps. 69.26, Exod. 22.23, Deut. 28.22, Deut. 28.35, Deut. 28.28, Lev. 26.29; ✥ Mic. 7.16-17, Deut. 29.19; [≅ Jer. 8.4 = Amos 8.14 ↔ Lev. 26.37]

QUOTATION	MT/TARGUM	BOWL	PUBLICATION	COMMENTS
Exod. 23.21	Exod. 23.21	M 164	Levene 2007	**CF:** שמאבר
ה שמי בקרבו	אֶל תַּמֵּר בְּפָנָיו וּשְׁמַע בְּקֹלוֹ אַל תַּמֵּר בּוֹ כִּי לֹא יִשָּׂא לְפִשְׁעֲכֶם כִּי שְׁמִי בְּקִרְבּוֹ			Other quotations: ✢ Isa. 50.11, Ps. 116.6, Ps. 91.11; Dan. 7.11 The bowl text also quotes m. Šebu. 4.13, and thus includes several other partial biblical quotations in the form of divine epithets

QUOTATION	MT/TARGUM	BOWL	PUBLICATION	COMMENTS
Lev. 26.29 ⁓ אכ[לו] בש[ר] בניכ[ם] ובכ[ם] ובשר בנתי[כ]ם ת[א]כלו	Lev. 26.29 וַאֲכַלְתֶּם בְּשַׂר בְּנֵיכֶם וּבְשַׂר בְּנֹתֵיכֶם תֹּאכֵלוּ	—	AMB 9	For cursing a named individual Other quotations: ❖ Ps. 69.24, Ps. 69.26, Exod. 22.23, Deut. 28.22, Deut. 28.35, Deut. 28.28, Lev. 26.29; ❖ Mic. 7.16-17, Deut. 29.19; [≅ Jer. 8.4 = Amos 8.14 ↔ Lev. 26.37]
Lev. 26.37 ↔ Jer. 8.4 ≡ Lev. 26.37 c Amos 8.14 הכה (אל) וכו(ל) אלו ולא אנה אלו אהלמלה אמונה מתחתה אסתה	Lev. 26.37 וְכָשְׁלוּ אִישׁ בְּאָחִיו כְּמִפְּנֵי חֶרֶב וְרֹדֵף אָיִן וְלֹא תִהְיֶה לָכֶם תְּקוּמָה לִפְנֵי אֹיְבֵיכֶם	—	AMB 9	See above

QUOTATION	MT/TARGUM	BOWL	PUBLICATION	COMMENTS
Num. 6.24-26 יברכך יהוה וישמרך {כן} יאר יהוה פניו אליך ויחנך ישא יהוה פניו אליך וישם לך שלום	Num. 6.24-26	BM 91765	Isbell 66 = CAMIB 26	✣ Song 3.7, Num. 6.24-26, Isa. 44.25
Num. 6.24-26 יברכך יהוה וישמרך ויברכהו יהוה וישמרהו ויברכני יהוה וישמרני וישמרו בלבבה וישמריה יאר יהוה פניו אליך ויחנך [variant list] ישא יהוה פניו אליך וישם לך שלום [variant list]	Num. 6.24-26	IM 76752	Faraj 2021	Lists of the beneficiary's livestock, family, and property inserted directly into the quotation after each verse Other quotations: Ps. 121.7; Ps 121.4
Num. 6.24-26 יברכך יהוה וישמרך יאר יהוה [אליך פניו] ויחנך ישא יהוה פניו אליך [וישם לך שלום]	Num. 6.24-26	MS 1927/9	Shaked 2005: 27	✣ Exod. 3.15, Num. 6.24-26 The text of the bowl is heavily effaced

Catalogue 67

	QUOTATION	MT/TARGUM	BOWL	PUBLICATION	COMMENTS
ℵ	Num. 6.24-26 יבר[כך] יהוה וישמרך [יהוה] יאר [אש]ר יהוה פניו אל[יך ויחנך] יהוה פנו אליך וישם לך שלום	Num. 6.24-26 יְבָרֶכְךָ יְהוָה וְיִשְׁמְרֶךָ׃ יָאֵר יְהוָה פָּנָיו אֵלֶיךָ וִיחֻנֶּךָּ׃ יִשָּׂא יְהוָה פָּנָיו אֵלֶיךָ וְיָשֵׂם לְךָ שָׁלוֹם׃	MS 2053/13	Shaked 2011: 209	Other quotations: Zech. 3.2 The writing is faded in parts
ℵ	Num. 9.23 על פי יהוה יחנו על פי יהוה יסעו את משמרת יהוה שמרו על פי יהוה ביד משה	Num. 9.23 עַל פִּי יְהוָה יַחֲנוּ וְעַל פִּי יְהוָה יִסָּעוּ אֶת מִשְׁמֶרֶת יְהוָה שָׁמָרוּ עַל פִּי יְהוָה בְּיַד מֹשֶׁה׃	Aaron B	Geller 1986: 108-109	✢ Zech. 3.2, Num. 9.23, Deut. 6.4 ⇄ Ps. 91.1
ℵ	Num. 9.23 על פי יהוה יחנו על פי יהוה יסעו את משמרת יהוה שמרו על פי יהוה ביד משה	Num. 9.23 עַל פִּי יְהוָה יַחֲנוּ וְעַל פִּי יְהוָה יִסָּעוּ אֶת מִשְׁמֶרֶת יְהוָה שָׁמָרוּ עַל פִּי יְהוָה בְּיַד מֹשֶׁה׃	Aaron F	Geller 1986: 115	
ℵ	Num. 9.23 ע[ל פי יהוה יחנו יהוה] על פי יהו[ה יס]עו את משמרת יהוה שמרו על פי יהוה ביד משה	Num. 9.23 עַל פִּי יְהוָה יַחֲנוּ וְעַל פִּי יְהוָה יִסָּעוּ אֶת מִשְׁמֶרֶת יְהוָה שָׁמָרוּ עַל פִּי יְהוָה בְּיַד מֹשֶׁה׃	MS 2053/41	JBA 31	

QUOTATION	MT/TARGUM	BOWL	PUBLICATION	COMMENTS
Num. 9.23	Num. 9.23	MS 2053/190	JBA 42	❖ Num. 9.23, Num. 10.36
על פ֯י יהוה יחנו על פ֯י {x} יהוה יסעו את משמרת יהוה שמרו על פי יהוה ביד משה	עַל־פִּ֤י יְהוָה֙ יַחֲנ֔וּ וְעַל־פִּ֥י יְהוָ֖ה יִסָּ֑עוּ אֶת־מִשְׁמֶ֤רֶת יְהוָה֙ שָׁמָ֔רוּ עַל־פִּ֥י יְהוָ֖ה בְּיַד־מֹשֶֽׁה			
Num. 9.23	Num. 9.23	MS 2053/126	JBA 73	
על פ֯י יהו֯ ׄיחנ֯ו֯ ו֯ע֯ל פ֯י יהו֯ יסעו את משמרת יהוה ש֯מ֯רו֯ [.]על פ֯י יה֯ו֯ ב֯י֯ד משה[ה]				
Num. 9.23	Num. 9.23	MS 2053/139	JBA 75	
על פ֯י יה֯ו֯ה יחנו ו֯ע֯[ל פ]י֯ יהו֯ [יסעו] א֯ת משמ֯ר֯ת י֯ה֯ו֯[ה] שמר֯ו֯ ע֯ל֯ פ֯י֯ יהו֯ה ב֯י֯ד משה				
Num. 9.23	Num. 9.23	MS 2053/196	JBA 103	❖ Num. 9.23, Zech. 3.2
על פ֯י יהוה֯ על פ<""">				Other quotations: ❖ Ps. 55.8, Ps. 91.7

QUOTATION	MT/TARGUM	BOWL	PUBLICATION	COMMENTS
Num. 9.23	Num. 9.23	M 6	Shaked 1995: 211-213	❖ Num. 9.23, Zech. 3.2, Ezek. 32.27, Ps. 91.11
על פי יהוה יחנו ועל פי יהוה יסעו את משמרת יהוה שמרו על פי יהוה ביד משה	עַל פִּי יְהוָה יַחֲנוּ וְעַל פִּי יְהוָה יִסָּעוּ אֶת מִשְׁמֶרֶת יְהוָה שָׁמָרוּ עַל פִּי יְהוָה בְּיַד מֹשֶׁה			
Num. 9.23	Num. 9.23	HS 3005	Ford/Morgenstern 2020: 19-20	
על פי יהוה יחנו ועל פי יהוה יסעו את משמרת יהוה שמרו על פי יהוה ביד משה	עַל פִּי יְהוָה יַחֲנוּ וְעַל פִּי יְהוָה יִסָּעוּ אֶת מִשְׁמֶרֶת יְהוָה שָׁמָרוּ עַל פִּי יְהוָה בְּיַד מֹשֶׁה			
Num. 9.23	Num. 9.23	HS 3022	Ford/Morgenstern 2020: 68-69	❖ Num. 11.2, Num. 9.23, Num. 12.13, Zech. 3.2
על פי יהוה יחנו ועל פי יהוה [את] משמרת [יהו]ה שמרו על פי יהוה ביד משה	עַל פִּי יְהוָה יַחֲנוּ וְעַל פִּי יְהוָה יִסָּעוּ אֶת מִשְׁמֶרֶת יְהוָה שָׁמָרוּ עַל פִּי יְהוָה בְּיַד מֹשֶׁה			
Num. 9.23	Num. 9.23	CBS 2952	AIT 5	❖ Num. 9.23, Zech. 3.2
על פי יהוה יחנו ועל פי יהוה יסעו את משמבת יהוה שמרו על פי יהוה ביד משה	עַל פִּי יְהוָה יַחֲנוּ וְעַל פִּי יְהוָה יִסָּעוּ אֶת מִשְׁמֶרֶת יְהוָה שָׁמָרוּ עַל פִּי יְהוָה בְּיַד מֹשֶׁה			

	QUOTATION	MT/TARGUM	BOWL	PUBLICATION	COMMENTS
ℵ	Num. 9.23	Num. 9.23	CBS 3997	AIT 26 = Shaked 1999: 194	✣ Deut. 6.4, Num. 9.23, Zech. 3.2 Other quotations: Hos. 2.2-4
	על פי יייי יסעו ונדר יייי על פי ב על פי יייי יחנו כל ימי אשר ישכן הענן (ד) ייייי	עַל פִּי יְהוָה יַחֲנוּ וְעַל פִּי יְהוָה יִסָּעוּ אֶת מִשְׁמֶרֶת יְהוָה שָׁמָרוּ עַל פִּי יְהוָה בְּיַד מֹשֶׁה			
ℵ	Num. 9.23	Num. 9.23	Einhorn 4	MSF 22	✣ Num. 9.23, Ezek. 32.27 The writing is extremely faded
	יהוה פי על ונדר יהוה פי על ישכן אשר ימי כל משה ביד יהוה פי על שמרו משמרת יהוה את ישעו[א ועל יהוה [הענן פי על]	עַל פִּי יְהוָה יַחֲנוּ וְעַל פִּי יְהוָה יִסָּעוּ אֶת מִשְׁמֶרֶת יְהוָה שָׁמָרוּ עַל פִּי יְהוָה בְּיַד מֹשֶׁה			
ℵ	Num. 10.35	Num. 10.35	HUJI Institute of Archaeology 1399	AMB 3	The final five letters of משנאיך are deliberately omitted from the quotation, likewise negating the threat of the beneficiary's enemies
	ויהי בנסע הארן ויאמר משה קומה יהוה ויפצו איביך וינסו משנאך [vacat] מלפניך	קוּמָה יְהוָה וְיָפֻצוּ אֹיְבֶיךָ וְיָנֻסוּ מְשַׂנְאֶיךָ מִפָּנֶיךָ			
ℵ	Num. 10.35	Num. 10.35	BM 91735	CAMIB 35	Other quotations: Isa. 44.25
	ויהי בנסע הארן ויאמר משה קומה יהוה ויפצו אויבוך וינוסו משנאיך מפנך	קוּמָה יְהוָה וְיָפֻצוּ אֹיְבֶיךָ וְיָנֻסוּ מְשַׂנְאֶיךָ מִפָּנֶיךָ			

QUOTATION	MT/TARGUM	BOWL	PUBLICATION	COMMENTS
Num. 10.35-36 ויהי בנסע הארן ויאמ[ר] משה קומ[ה] יה[וה ויפצו] איביך [וינס]ו משנ[איך מפניך] ובנ[ח]ה יאמר שוב[ה יהוה רבבות] אלפי ישראל	Num. 10.35-36 וַיְהִי בִּנְסֹעַ הָאָרֹן וַיֹּאמֶר מֹשֶׁה קוּמָה יְהוָה וְיָפֻצוּ אֹיְבֶיךָ וְיָנֻסוּ מְשַׂנְאֶיךָ מִפָּנֶיךָ וּבְנֻחֹה יֹאמַר שׁוּבָה יְהוָה רִבְבוֹת אַלְפֵי יִשְׂרָאֵל	MS 2053/7	Bohak 2012: 47	CF: באמרה Other quotations: Zech. 3.2
Num. 10.36	Num. 10.36 וּבְנֻחֹה יֹאמַר שׁוּבָה יְהוָה רִבְבוֹת אַלְפֵי יִשְׂרָאֵל	MS 2053/190	JBA 42	✣ Num. 9.23, Num. 10.36
Num. 11.2 ו]יצעק[ו אל מ]ה העם אל מש[ה ואת יעתר יהוה אל הש[ו	Num. 11.2 וַיִּצְעַק הָעָם אֶל מֹשֶׁה וַיִּתְפַּלֵּל מֹשֶׁה אֶל יְהוָה וַתִּשְׁקַע הָאֵשׁ	HS 3022	Ford/Morgenstern 2020: 68-69	✣ Num. 11.2, Num. 9.23, Num. 12.13, Zech. 3.2

	QUOTATION	MT/TARGUM	BOWL	PUBLICATION	COMMENTS
ℵ	Num. 12.13 ויצעק משה אל יהוה לאמר אל נא רפא נא לה	Num. 12.13 וַיִּצְעַק מֹשֶׁה אֶל יְהוָה לֵאמֹר אֵל נָא רְפָא נָא לָהּ	HS 3022	Ford/Morgenstern 2020: 68-69	✥ Num. 11.2, Num. 9.23, Num. 12.13, Zech. 3.2
ℵ	Num. 12.13 ויצ[עק] משה אל יהוה לאמר אל נא רפא נא לה	Num. 12.13 וַיִּצְעַק מֹשֶׁה אֶל יְהוָה לֵאמֹר אֵל נָא רְפָא נָא לָהּ	MS 2053/218	JBA 108	✥ Zech. 3.2, Num. 12.13
ℵ	Num. 14.9 אך את יהוה אל תמרדו ואתם אל תיראו את עם הארץ (ונמה ל) לחמנו הם סר צלם מעליהם ויהוה אתנו אל תיראום	Num. 14.9 אַךְ בַּיהוָה אַל תִּמְרֹדוּ וְאַתֶּם אַל תִּירְאוּ אֶת עַם הָאָרֶץ כִּי לַחְמֵנוּ הֵם סָר צִלָּם מֵעֲלֵיהֶם וַיהוָה אִתָּנוּ אַל תִּירָאֻם	M 142	Corpus: 93-94	✥ Num. 32.22, Num. 14.9 Other quotations: Isa. 40.31

Catalogue

QUOTATION	MT/TARGUM	BOWL	PUBLICATION	COMMENTS
Num. 32.22	Num. 32.22	M 142	Corpus: 93-94	✜ Num. 32.22, Num. 14.9 Other quotations: Isa. 40.31
יהוה יהוה נפל יראה ונשבנהו ביהוה] םייב מויה מריהו ונשלם אתה יראה יהוה[יה ישראלה יהוה נפל יהוה מכה	יראו יהוה נפל יראה ונשבנהו ביהוה םייב מריהו ונשלם אתה יראה יהוה יהוה ישראלה יהוה נפל יהוה מכה			
Deut. 6.4	Deut. 6.4	JNF 124	Ford 2016: 153-154	✜ Deut. 6.4, Ps. 91.1, Exod. 14.31 Followed by אחד הוא בשמים, cf. the Haggadah song ʾEḥad Mi Yodeʿa
שמע ישראל יהוה אלהינו יהוה אחד	שמע ישראל יהוה אלהינו יהוה אחד			
Deut. 6.4	Deut. 6.4	CBS 3997	AIT 26 = Shaked 1999: 194	✜ Deut. 6.4, Num. 9.23, Zech. 3.2 Other quotations: Hos. 2.2-4
שמע ישראל יהוה אלהינו ״״ יהוה אחד	שמע ישראל יהוה אלהינו יהוה אחד			
Deut. 6.4	Deut. 6.4	De Menil	Isbell 1976: 16-20	
שמע ישראל יהוה אלהינו יהוה אח[ד]	שמע ישראל יהוה אלהינו יהוה אחד			

QUOTATION	MT/TARGUM	BOWL	PUBLICATION	COMMENTS
Deut. 6.4 שְׁמַע יִשְׂרָאֵל] יְהוָה אֱלֹהֵינוּ [יְהוָה אֶחָד	Deut. 6.4 שְׁמַע יִשְׂרָאֵל יְהוָה אֱלֹהֵינוּ יְהוָה אֶחָד	T 27987	Misgav 2018	The opening lines of the text are effaced. It is unclear whether the bowl quotes only the first two words of Deut. 6.4 or whether it quotes the whole verse (though the lacuna appears large enough) Other quotations: Zech. 3.2
Deut. 6.4 שְׁמַע יִשְׂרָ[אֵל] יְהוָה אֱלֹהֵינוּ [יְהוָה אֶחָד	Deut. 6.4 שְׁמַע יִשְׂרָאֵל יְהוָה אֱלֹהֵינוּ יְהוָה אֶחָד	—	Müller-Kessler 2013	A large portion of the text is effaced
Deut. 6.4 ⇄ Ps. 91.1[1] שמע ישראל יהוה אלהינו יהוה אחד שוכן בסתר עליון יהוה אלהינו	Deut. 6.4 שְׁמַע יִשְׂרָאֵל יְהוָה אֱלֹהֵינוּ יְהוָה אֶחָד	JHMB 242/1	AMB 11	⸙ Zech. 3.2, Deut. 6.4 ⇄ Ps. 91.1

	QUOTATION	MT/TARGUM	BOWL	PUBLICATION	COMMENTS
I	Deut. 6.4 ⇄ Ps. 91.1 [יהוה]ב ישראל שמע שמע [יי]ה אלהינו יהוה יהוה ישכן עליון בסתר יושב אחד	Deut. 6.4 שְׁמַע יִשְׂרָאֵל יְהוָה אֱלֹהֵינוּ יְהוָה אֶחָד	Louvre AOD 361	Schwab O = Schwab 1891: 592	Other quotations: Zech. 3.2 Partial edition of the bowl text
I	Deut. 6.4 ⇄ Ps. 91.1 שמע ישראל יהוה בסתר יהוה ישכן עליון אלהינו יהוה אחד יהיה בצל ויהוה ד(ש)	Deut. 6.4 שְׁמַע יִשְׂרָאֵל יְהוָה אֱלֹהֵינוּ יְהוָה אֶחָד	Aaron B	Geller 1986: 108-109	✣ Zech. 3.2, Num. 9.23, Deut. 6.4 ⇄ Ps. 91.1
I P	Deut. 6.4 ⇄ Ps. 91.1 שמע ישראל יהוה בסתר אֶחָד יְהוָה אֱלֹהֵינוּ יְהוָה יִשְׂרָאֵל שְׁמַע	Deut. 6.4	ZRL 48	Gordon 1978: 233	Other quotations: Zech. 3.2

QUOTATION	MT/TARGUM	BOWL	PUBLICATION	COMMENTS
Deut. 6.4-9	Deut. 6.4-9	VA 3854	Levene 2003: 105-106	✥ Deut. 6.4-9, Deut. 11.13-21 Duplicate of VA 3853, though VA 3853 (accidentally) omits Deut. 6.7-8 With liturgical response after Deut. 6.4

Catalogue

QUOTATION	MT/TARGUM	BOWL	PUBLICATION	COMMENTS
6 Deut. 6.4-9 שמע ישראל יהוה אלוהינו יהוה אחד ברוך שם כבוד מלכותו לעולם ועד ואה(א)בת את יהוה אלהיך {אל(x)הנ} בכל לבבך ובכל נפשך ובכל מאדך [והיו] הדברים האלה על לבבך ושנ[נ]תם לבניך ודברת בם {ודב} בלכתך	Deut. 6.4-9 שְׁמַע יִשְׂרָאֵל יְהוָה אֱלֹהֵינוּ יְהוָה אֶחָד וְאָהַבְתָּ אֵת יְהוָה אֱלֹהֶיךָ בְּכָל לְבָבְךָ וּבְכָל נַפְשְׁךָ וּבְכָל מְאֹדֶךָ וְהָיוּ הַדְּבָרִים הָאֵלֶּה אֲשֶׁר אָנֹכִי מְצַוְּךָ הַיּוֹם עַל לְבָבֶךָ וְשִׁנַּנְתָּם לְבָנֶיךָ וְדִבַּרְתָּ בָּם בְּשִׁבְתְּךָ בְּבֵיתֶךָ וּבְלֶכְתְּךָ בַדֶּרֶךְ וּבְשָׁכְבְּךָ וּבְקוּמֶךָ וּקְשַׁרְתָּם לְאוֹת עַל יָדֶךָ וְהָיוּ לְטֹטָפֹת בֵּין עֵינֶיךָ וּכְתַבְתָּם עַל מְזוּזֹת בֵּיתֶךָ וּבִשְׁעָרֶיךָ	VA 3853	Levene 2003: 107-108	✣ Deut. 6.4-9, Deut. 11.13-21 Duplicate of VA 3854, though VA 3853 (accidentally) omits Deut. 6.7-8 With liturgical response after Deut. 6.4

QUOTATION	MT/TARGUM	BOWL	PUBLICATION	COMMENTS
Deut. 6.4-9 שמע ישראל יהוה אלהינו יהוה אחד ואהבת את יהוה אלהיך בכל לבבך ובכל נפשך ובכל מאדך והיו הדברים האלה אשר אנכי מצוך היום על לבבך ושננתם לבניך ודברת בם בשבתך בבית[ך] ובלכתך בדרך ובשכבך ובקומך וקשרתם לאות על ידך והיו לטטפת(?) בין עיניך וכתבתם על מזזות בית[ך] ובשעריך [6] שמע ישראל יהוה אלה(?)ינו יהוה אח[ד] יהוה	Deut. 6.4-9	HS 3027	Ford/Morgenstern 2020: 86-87	✣ Deut. 6.4-9, Deut. 11.13-14a Deut. 6.4 is repeated at the end of the bowl text (l. 6)
Deut. 6.19 להדף את כל (א)ויבי(ך) מפניך כאשר דבר יהוה	Deut. 6.19 להדֹף אֶת־כל־אֹיְבֶיךָ מִפָּנֶיךָ כַּאֲשֶׁר דִּבֶּר יהוה	VA 2484	Curses: 22-24	For returning a רוח or jackal-spirit to several named individuals

QUOTATION	MT/TARGUM	BOWL	PUBLICATION	COMMENTS
א Deut. 10.17 = Neh 9.32 E אל הגבר הגבור והנורא P	Deut. 10.17 כִּי יְהוָה אֱלֹהֵיכֶם הוּא אֱלֹהֵי הָאֱלֹהִים וַאֲדֹנֵי הָאֲדֹנִים הָאֵל הַגָּדֹל הַגִּבֹּר וְהַנּוֹרָא	M 102	Curses: 108-109	For overturning and returning curses upon two/three named individuals EC *Shemaʿ*, First Blessing Invoked as name of power: בשם ... ונשמע
♆ Deut. 11.13-14 S Deut. 11.13-14 P [היה] אם שמע אל מצות יהוה אשר אנכי מצוה אתכם [ה]יום לאהבה את יהוה אלהיכם ולעבדו בכל לבבכם ובכל נפשכם ונתתי מטר ארצכם	Deut. 11.13-14 וְהָיָה אִם־שָׁמֹעַ תִּשְׁמְעוּ אֶל־מִצְוֺתַי אֲשֶׁר אָנֹכִי מְצַוֶּה אֶתְכֶם הַיּוֹם לְאַהֲבָה אֶת־יְהוָה אֱלֹהֵיכֶם וּלְעָבְדוֹ בְּכָל־לְבַבְכֶם וּבְכָל־נַפְשְׁכֶם וְנָתַתִּי מְטַר־אַרְצְכֶם בְּעִתּוֹ יוֹרֶה וּמַלְקוֹשׁ	HS 3027	Ford/Morgenstern 2020: 86-87	✤ Deut. 6.4-9, Deut. 11.13-14a Deut. 6.4 is repeated at the end of the bowl text

QUOTATION	MT/TARGUM	BOWL	PUBLICATION	COMMENTS
Deut. 11.13-21	Deut. 11.13-21	VA 3854	Levene 2003: 105-106	✣ Deut. 6.4-9, Deut. 11.13-21 Duplicate of VA 3853 Lack of writing space is almost certainly why Deut. 11.21b is missing

Catalogue

QUOTATION	MT/TARGUM	BOWL	PUBLICATION	COMMENTS
על הלא יהוה את ממטר משבצו כל {ו} הככה לצבעם ועל אומץ כח גבעתן וכל אמץ אדם אומץ דמן עד על מעשה ידו וכל דרך איש ישלם לו	על הלא יהוה את ממטר משבצו כל ו הככה לצבעם ועל אומץ כח גבעתן וכל אמץ אדם אומץ דמן עד על מעשה ידו וכל דרך איש ישלם לו	נשמטם על נשאלה ואנכלם לשם כחו ככה ונשומע אמר ונתן בידה ונתנתי אתם בידכם ויכם		
ובטהרון [ולו כל] ובתהומא על משות בתר	ובטהרון ולו כל ובתהומא על משות בתר	וכעמחין ובתהומא על משות בתר		
נשמטם על נשאלך אחר טבעבם כחו ככה ככה ונשומע ואנכלם ככה אתר בידכם כחכם כל	נשמטם על נשאלך אחר טבעבם כחו ככה ככה ונשומע ואנכלם ככה אתר בידכם כחכם כל	נשמטם על נשאלך <אנכלם לשם כחו ככה> <וכמחום אמר כחו ככה> נשל דא<רעא> ידכן לי כתב על ואנכלם ככה אתר בידכם כחכם כל		

QUOTATION	MT/TARGUM	BOWL	PUBLICATION	COMMENTS
Deut. 11.13-21	Deut. 11.13-21	VA 3853	Levene 2003: 107-108	✣ Deut. 6.4-9, Deut. 11.13-21 Duplicate of VA 3854 Lack of writing space is almost certainly why Deut. 11.21 is missing

Catalogue 83

QUOTATION	MT/TARGUM	BOWL	PUBLICATION	COMMENTS

QUOTATION	MT/TARGUM	BOWL	PUBLICATION	COMMENTS
Deut. 28.22 יַכְּכָה יְהוָה בַּשַּׁחֶפֶת וּבַקַּדַּחַת וּבַדַּלֶּקֶת וּבַחַרְחֻר וּבַחֶרֶב וּבַשִּׁדָּפוֹן וּבַיֵּרָקוֹן וּרְדָפוּךָ עַד אָבְדֶךָ	Deut. 28.22 יִמְחֵינָךְ יְיָ בְּשַׁחֶפְתָּא וּבְאִישָׁתָא וּבִדְלֶקְתָּא וּבְחַמְטָא וּבְקַטָּלָא וּבְשִׁדְפוֹנָא וּבְיַרְקוֹנָא וְיִרְדְּפוּנָךְ עַד דְּתֵיבַד	—	AMB 9	For cursing a named individual Cf: יקום עליה יהוה בר Other quotations: ❖ Ps. 69.24, Ps. 69.26, Exod. 22.23, Deut. 28.22, Deut. 28.35, Deut. 28.28, Lev. 26.29; ❖ Mic. 7.16-17, Deut. 29.19; [≅ Jer. 8.4 = Amos 8.14 ↔ Lev. 26.37]
Deut. 28.28 יַכְּכָה יְהוָה בְּשִׁגָּעוֹן וּבְעִוָּרוֹן וּבְתִמְהוֹן [לבב]	Deut. 28.28 יִמְחֵינָךְ יְיָ בְּשִׁגְעוֹנָא וּבְסַמְיוּתָא וּבְתִמְהוֹן לִבָּא	—	AMB 9	See above

QUOTATION	MT/TARGUM	BOWL	PUBLICATION	COMMENTS
Deut. 28.35	Deut. 28.35	—	AMB 9	See above
הנה יהוה [מכה ב]על על ברכים ועל שקים אשר לא תוכל להרפא מכף רגלך {ו}עד קדקדך	יַכְּכָה יְהוָה בִּשְׁחִין רָע עַל־הַבִּרְכַּיִם וְעַל־הַשֹּׁקַיִם אֲשֶׁר לֹא־תוּכַל לְהֵרָפֵא מִכַּף רַגְלְךָ וְעַד קָדְקֳדֶךָ			
Deut. 28.57	Deut. 28.57	MS 2053/249	JBA 46	**CF:** הוה דנה תקבלה לטמיא דהב יתיב על לבה ודה דחויא דמיזא וקטרן בנבה
והרע בעיניה באיש חיקה ובבנה ובבתה ובשליתה היוצת מבין רגליה ובבניה אשר תלד כי תאכלם בחסר כל בסתר במצור ובמצוק אשר יציק לך איביך בשעריך	וְהָרַע בְּעֵינֶיהָ בְּאִישׁ חֵיקָהּ וּבִבְנָהּ וּבְבִתָּהּ וּבְשִׁלְיָתָהּ הַיּוֹצֵת מִבֵּין רַגְלֶיהָ וּבְבָנֶיהָ אֲשֶׁר תֵּלֵד כִּי־תֹאכְלֵם בְּחֹסֶר־כֹּל בַּסָּתֶר בְּמָצוֹר וּבְמָצוֹק אֲשֶׁר יָצִיק לְךָ אֹיִבְךָ בִּשְׁעָרֶיךָ			

QUOTATION	MT/TARGUM	BOWL	PUBLICATION	COMMENTS
Deut. 29.19	Deut. 29.19	—	AMB 9	For cursing a named individual
לֹא(1) [אָבָה] ייי סְלֹחַ לֹו (פ) כִּי אָז יֶעְשַׁן אַף(1) ייי וְקִנְאָתוֹ בָּאִישׁ הַהוּא [הַהֲבוּרָה] בּוֹ כָל הָאָלָה הַכְּתוּבָה בַּסֵּפֶר הַזֶּה וּמָחָה ייי [הוהה] אֶת שְׁמוֹ מִתַּחַת הַשָּׁמַיִם	לָא יֵיבֵי יְיָ לְמִשְׁבַּק לֵיהּ אֲרוּם בְּכֵן יִתְקוֹף רוּגְזָא דַייָ וְחֵמְתֵיהּ בְּגַבְרָא הַהוּא וִידַבְּקוּן בֵּיהּ כָּל לְוָטַיָא דִכְתִיבִין בְּסִפְרָא הָדֵין וְיִמְחוֹק יְיָ יָת שְׁמֵיהּ מִתְּחוֹת שְׁמַיָּא			Other quotations: ❖ Ps. 69.24, Ps. 69.26, Exod. 22.23, Deut. 28.22, Deut. 28.35, Deut. 28.28, Lev. 26.29; ❖ Mic. 7.16-17, Deut. 29.19; [≅ Jer. 8.4 = Amos 8.14 ↔ Lev. 26.37]

QUOTATION	MT/TARGUM	BOWL	PUBLICATION	COMMENTS
࠶ Deut. 29.22 גפרית ומלח שרפה כל ארצה לא תזרע ולא תצמח ולא יעלה בה כל עשב כמהפכת סדם ועמרה אדמה וצביים אשר הפך יהוה באפו ובחמתו	Deut. 29.22 גָּפְרִית וָמֶלַח שְׂרֵפָה כָל־אַרְצָהּ לֹא תִזָּרַע וְלֹא תַצְמִחַ וְלֹא־יַעֲלֶה בָהּ כָּל־עֵשֶׂב כְּמַהְפֵּכַת סְדֹם וַעֲמֹרָה אַדְמָה וּצְבֹיִים אֲשֶׁר הָפַךְ יְהוָה בְּאַפּוֹ וּבַחֲמָתוֹ	BM 91767	Curses: 119-120 = CAMIB 40	For cursing a named individual Written on the exterior of the bowl Repeated in reverse order Other quotations: Deut. 29.27
࠶ Deut. 29.27 = Jer 21.5 P ויתשם יהוה מעל אדמתם באף ובחמה ובקצף גדול וישלכם	Deut. 29.27 וַיִּתְּשֵׁם יְהוָה מֵעַל אַדְמָתָם בְּאַף וּבְחֵמָה וּבְקֶצֶף גָּדוֹל וַיַּשְׁלִכֵם אֶל־אֶרֶץ אַחֶרֶת כַּיּוֹם הַזֶּה	BM 91767	Curses: 119-120 = CAMIB 40	For cursing a named individual Other quotations: Deut. 29.22

QUOTATION	MT/TARGUM	BOWL	PUBLICATION	COMMENTS
ℵ Deut. 29.27 = Jer 21.5 ס אֶת יְהוָה אֵת הָמְרַתּ בָּם לֵמָה יְהוָה מָשַׁרַע יָצֶא עָצֶן אֶל מְקוֹמוֹת אֶל יְהוָה אֲשֶׁר הִמְרוּ יְהוָה אֲחֵרִים אֵין	Deut. 29.27	BM 91770	Curses: 123 = CAMIB 43	For cursing a named individual
Deut. 32.3 בִּי יַד יְהוָה אֶקְרָא שֵׁם 'ה וַהֲדָרוֹת	Deut. 32.3 לָא 'בָה אַקְרָא יְהוָה שָׁ 'בָה וַהֲדָרוֹת	M1	Shaked 1995: 207	Follows an invocation of God. Other quotations: ❖ Ezek. 1.27 ↔ Ezek. 1.5; Isa. 6.3
1 Sam. 2.2 אֵין קָדוֹשׁ כ יְהוָה כִי אֵין בִּלְתָּ וְאֵין צוּר כֵּאלֹהִינוּ	1 Sam. 2.2 אֵין קָדוֹשׁ [יהוה] בַּה 'יִ אֵין בַּלֵּתָךְ וְאֵין תַּקִיף כֵּאלֹהִינוּ	Moriah 2	Gordon 1984: 238	❖ 1 Sam. 2.2, Ps. 86.17 Tetragrammaton (and preposition) enclosed in a cartouche

QUOTATION	MT/TARGUM	BOWL	PUBLICATION	COMMENTS
א 1 Sam. 17.45 ⇌ Isa. 6.3	1 Sam. 17.45	M 117	Corpus: 77	Invoked as name of power:
C				בשמיה ד
P קדוש קדוש קדוש יהוה צבאות אלהי ישראל מרעמה יהבא	הָאתָּה בָּא אֵלַי בְּחֶרֶב וּבַחֲנִית וּבְכִידוֹן וְאָנֹכִי בָא־אֵלֶיךָ בְּשֵׁם יְהוָה צְבָאוֹת אֱלֹהֵי מַעַרְכוֹת יִשְׂרָאֵל אֲשֶׁר חֵרַפְתָּ׃			Other quotations: Isa. 37.16
א 2 Kgs 19.15	2 Kgs 19.15	VA 2416	Curses: 46-47	For returning curses upon a named individual
E יהוה אלהי ישראל ישב הכרובים	יְהוָה אֱלֹהֵי יִשְׂרָאֵל יֹשֵׁב הַכְּרֻבִים אַתָּה־הוּא הָאֱלֹהִים לְבַדְּךָ לְכֹל מַמְלְכוֹת הָאָרֶץ אַתָּה עָשִׂיתָ אֶת־הַשָּׁמַיִם וְאֶת־הָאָרֶץ׃			
P				EC
E Isa. 6.3	Isa. 6.3	S-446	SHM 4	EC
P קדוש קדוש קדוש יהוה צבאות מלא כל הארץ כבודו	קָדוֹשׁ קָדוֹשׁ קָדוֹשׁ יְהוָה צְבָאוֹת מְלֹא כָל־הָאָרֶץ כְּבוֹדוֹ׃			

QUOTATION	MT/TARGUM	BOWL	PUBLICATION	COMMENTS
E Isa. 6.3	Isa. 6.3	Harvard ANE Museum 1899.2.658	Isbell 33	Invoked as name of power: ב[שם]
P קד[וש] קדוש קדוש יהוה צבאות מלא כל הארץ כבודו	קָדוֹשׁ קָדוֹשׁ קָדוֹשׁ יְהוָה צְבָאוֹת מְלֹא כָל־הָאָרֶץ כְּבוֹדוֹ			
E Isa. 6.3	Isa. 6.3	M1	Shaked 1995: 207	Invoked as name of power: הן הוא שמע דהקדוש ואמר קדושיו Underlined
P קדוש קדוש קדוש יהוה צבאות מלא כל הארץ כבודו	קָדוֹשׁ קָדוֹשׁ קָדוֹשׁ יְהוָה צְבָאוֹת מְלֹא כָל־הָאָרֶץ כְּבוֹדוֹ			Other quotations: Deut. 32.3; ✧ Ezek. 1.27 ↔ Ezek. 1.5
Isa. 6.3	Isa. 6.3	MS 1927/50	JBA 116	Other quotations: Exod. 14.31, Ps. 114.3 (T)
קדוש ק[דוש ק]דוש יה[וה] צבאות מלא כל הארץ כ[ב]ודו	קָדוֹשׁ קָדוֹשׁ קָדוֹשׁ יְהוָה צְבָאוֹת מְלֹא כָל־הָאָרֶץ כְּבוֹדוֹ			

QUOTATION	MT/TARGUM	BOWL	PUBLICATION	COMMENTS
Isa. 6.3	Isa. 6.3	MS 2053/159	Corpus: 100–102	✣ Isa. 6.3 (3x), Exod. 15.16 (3x), Exod. 15.18 (3x)
[וקר]א זה אל [זה ואמ]ר קדוש קדוש קדוש יהוה צבאות כל [א]רץ יקר[א] זה אל זה קדוש קדוש קדוש יהוה צבאות מלא כל הארץ כבודו יהוה קדוש קדוש קדוש יהוה צבאות מלא כל הארץ כבוד[ו] יהוה [ק]דן [א]ל זה ואמר קדוש קדוש קדוש יהוה צבאות מלא כל הארץ כבוד[ו]	וְקָרָא זֶה אֶל זֶה וְאָמַר קָדוֹשׁ קָדוֹשׁ קָדוֹשׁ יְהוָה צְבָאוֹת מְלֹא כָל הָאָרֶץ כְּבוֹדוֹ			
c Isa. 6.3 ⇄ 1 Sam 17.45 p	Isa. 6.3	M 117	Corpus: 77	Invoked as name of power: בשמיה ד Other quotations: Isa. 37.16
קדוש קדוש קדוש יהוה צבאות אלהא ישראל מלכא יהוה צבאות	קָדוֹשׁ קָדוֹשׁ קָדוֹשׁ יְהוָה צְבָאוֹת מְלֹא כָל הָאָרֶץ כְּבוֹדוֹ			
Isa. 12.3	Isa. 12.3	MS 2053/125	JBA 90	
ושאבתם מים בשאבה ממעייני הישועה	וּשְׁאַבְתֶּם מַיִם בְּשָׂשׂוֹן מִמַּעַיְנֵי הַיְשׁוּעָה			

	QUOTATION	MT/TARGUM	BOWL	PUBLICATION	COMMENTS
E	Isa. 37.16	Isa 37.16	M 117	Corpus: 77	Invoked as a name of power: בשם
P	יהוה צבאות אלהי ישראל יושב הכרובים	יְהוָה צְבָאוֹת אֱלֹהֵי יִשְׂרָאֵל ישֵׁב הַכְּרֻבִים אַתָּה־הוּא הָאֱלֹהִים לְבַדְּךָ לְכֹל מַמְלְכוֹת הָאָרֶץ אַתָּה עָשִׂיתָ אֶת־הַשָּׁמַיִם וְאֶת־הָאָרֶץ			The first four lines of the bowl text are written in Mishnaic Hebrew, while a targumic equivalent appears in l. 5: יהוה צבאות אלהא (Tg. Ps-J.) דישראל Other quotations: Isa. 6.3 ⇌ 1 Sam. 17.45
E	Isa. 37.16	Isa 37.16	IM 212092	Al-Jubouri 2013	Invoked as a name of power: בשם
P	יהוה צבאות אלהי ישראל יושב הכרובים	יְהוָה צְבָאוֹת אֱלֹהֵי יִשְׂרָאֵל ישֵׁב הַכְּרֻבִים אַתָּה־הוּא הָאֱלֹהִים לְבַדְּךָ לְכֹל מַמְלְכוֹת הָאָרֶץ אַתָּה עָשִׂיתָ אֶת־הַשָּׁמַיִם וְאֶת־הָאָרֶץ			

	QUOTATION	MT/TARGUM	BOWL	PUBLICATION	COMMENTS
E	Isa. 37.16	Isa. 37.16	IM 212093	Al-Jubouri 2015	Invoked as a name of power: בשום
P	יהוה צבאות אלהי ישראל ישב הכרובים	יְהוָה צְבָאוֹת אֱלֹהֵי יִשְׂרָאֵל יֹשֵׁב הַכְּרֻבִים אַתָּה־הוּא הָאֱלֹהִים לְבַדְּךָ לְכֹל מַמְלְכוֹת הָאָרֶץ אַתָּה עָשִׂיתָ אֶת־הַשָּׁמַיִם וְאֶת־הָאָרֶץ			
E	Isa. 37.16	Isa. 37.16	IM 212103	Al-Jubouri 2011	Invoked as a name of power: בשום
P	יהוה צבאות אלהי ישראל ישב הכרובים	יְהוָה צְבָאוֹת אֱלֹהֵי יִשְׂרָאֵל יֹשֵׁב הַכְּרֻבִים אַתָּה־הוּא הָאֱלֹהִים לְבַדְּךָ לְכֹל מַמְלְכוֹת הָאָרֶץ אַתָּה עָשִׂיתָ אֶת־הַשָּׁמַיִם וְאֶת־הָאָרֶץ			

QUOTATION	MT/TARGUM	BOWL	PUBLICATION	COMMENTS
Isa. 40.6-8 קול אמר קרא ואמר מה אקרא כל הבשר חציר וכל חסדו כציץ השדה יבש חציר נבל ציץ כי רוח יהוה נשבה בו אכן חציר העם יבש חציר נבל ציץ ודבר [יהוה] אלהינו יקום לעלם	Isa. 40.6-8	—	Herman 2021	Tetragrammaton and "but the word of our God" enclosed in a cartouche
Isa. 40.12 מי מדד בשעלו מים ושמים בזרת תכן וכל בשלש עפר הארץ ושקל {בפלס} הרים ובקעות במאזנים	Isa. 40.12	MMA 86.11.259	AMB 12b	

	QUOTATION	MT/TARGUM	BOWL	PUBLICATION	COMMENTS
P	Isa. 40.12 בז[ש]ל[ש] עפר הארץ ו[ם] ה בכלם [ם]ילנג[ת] [...]	Isa. 40.12 מִי־מָדַד בְּשָׁעֳלוֹ מַיִם וְשָׁמַיִם בַּזֶּרֶת תִּכֵּן וְכָל בַּשָּׁלִשׁ עֲפַר הָאָרֶץ וְשָׁקַל בַּפֶּלֶס הָרִים וּגְבָעוֹת בְּמֹאזְנָיִם	BM 117869+ BM 117870+ BM 117871	CAMIB 71+ CAMIB 72+ CAMIB 73	Only several fragments of the bowl are preserved Other quotations: Gen. 49.22
P	Isa. 40.12 בם שמול מדד בשעלו מים	Isa. 40.12 מִי־מָדַד בְּשָׁעֳלוֹ מַיִם וְשָׁמַיִם בַּזֶּרֶת תִּכֵּן וְכָל בַּשָּׁלִשׁ עֲפַר הָאָרֶץ וְשָׁקַל בַּפֶּלֶס הָרִים וּגְבָעוֹת בְּמֹאזְנָיִם	JNL Heb. 4 6079	AMB 12a	Other quotations: Song 3.7-8
P	Isa. 40.12 מהמדד מדד בשעלו מים	Isa. 40.12 מִי־מָדַד בְּשָׁעֳלוֹ מַיִם וְשָׁמַיִם בַּזֶּרֶת תִּכֵּן וְכָל בַּשָּׁלִשׁ עֲפַר הָאָרֶץ וְשָׁקַל בַּפֶּלֶס הָרִים וּגְבָעוֹת בְּמֹאזְנָיִם	HS 3003	Ford/Morgenstern 2020: 14-15	

QUOTATION	MT/TARGUM	BOWL	PUBLICATION	COMMENTS
P Isa. 40.12 במשעלו תכן מים	Isa. 40.12 מִי־מָדַד בְּשָׁעֳלוֹ מַיִם וְשָׁמַיִם בַּזֶּרֶת תִּכֵּן וְכָל בַּשָּׁלִשׁ עֲפַר הָאָרֶץ וְשָׁקַל בַּפֶּלֶס הָרִים וּגְבָעוֹת בְּמֹאזְנָיִם	IM 114987	ZHS 4a	
P Isa. 40.12 במשעלו תכן מים	Isa. 40.12 מִי־מָדַד בְּשָׁעֳלוֹ מַיִם וְשָׁמַיִם בַּזֶּרֶת תִּכֵּן וְכָל בַּשָּׁלִשׁ עֲפַר הָאָרֶץ וְשָׁקַל בַּפֶּלֶס הָרִים וּגְבָעוֹת בְּמֹאזְנָיִם	XI-t 5178	Müller-Kessler 1994: 6 (B1)	
P Isa. 40.12 במשעלו תכן מים	Isa. 40.12 מִי־מָדַד בְּשָׁעֳלוֹ מַיִם וְשָׁמַיִם בַּזֶּרֶת תִּכֵּן וְכָל בַּשָּׁלִשׁ עֲפַר הָאָרֶץ וְשָׁקַל בַּפֶּלֶס הָרִים וּגְבָעוֹת בְּמֹאזְנָיִם	—	Müller-Kessler 1994: 6 (B2)	

Catalogue

QUOTATION	MT/TARGUM	BOWL	PUBLICATION	COMMENTS
Isa. 40.31	Isa. 40.31	MS 1911/1	JBA 65	'For (the) livelihood' (למזוני) of the beneficiary
וקוי יהוה יחליפו כח יעלו אבר כנשרים ירצו ולא יגעו ילכו ולא ייעפו	וּדְסַבְרוּ לְמֵימְרָא דַייָ יַחְלְפוּן חֵיל יִתְחַדַּת עוּלֵימְהוֹן הֵיךְ גַּדְפִין סָלְקִין עַל נִשְׁרִין יִרְהֲטוּן וְלָא יִלְאוּן יְהָכוּן וְלָא יִשְׁתַּלְהוּן			❖ Exod. 3.15, Isa. 40.31 Other quotations: ❖ Isa. 60.11 ↔ Gen. 27.28
Isa. 40.31	Isa. 40.31	MS 2053/56	JBA 67	❖ Exod. 3.15, Isa. 40.31 Other quotations: ❖ Isa. 60.11 ↔ Gen. 27.28; ❖ Ps. 121.7-8, Zech. 3.2
וקוי יהוה יח[ל]י[פ]ו כ[ח] יעלו אבר כנ[ש]רים י[רו]צו ו[י]לכו [ו]לא [י]עיפ[ו]	וּדְסַבְרוּ לְמֵימְרָא דַייָ יַחְלְפוּן חֵיל יִתְחַדַּת עוּלֵימְהוֹן הֵיךְ גַּדְפִין סָלְקִין עַל נִשְׁרִין יִרְהֲטוּן וְלָא יִלְאוּן יְהָכוּן וְלָא יִשְׁתַּלְהוּן			
Isa. 40.31	Isa. 40.31	MS 2053/69	JBA 95	❖ Exod. 3.15, Isa. 40.31 Other quotations: ❖ Isa. 60.11 ↔ Gen. 27.28
וקוי יהוה יח[לי]פו כח ילכ[ו] ר[כ]א אבר כנשרים יצרו ולא ייעפו	וּדְסַבְרוּ לְמֵימְרָא דַייָ יַחְלְפוּן חֵיל יִתְחַדַּת עוּלֵימְהוֹן הֵיךְ גַּדְפִין סָלְקִין עַל נִשְׁרִין יִרְהֲטוּן וְלָא יִלְאוּן יְהָכוּן וְלָא יִשְׁתַּלְהוּן			

QUOTATION	MT/TARGUM	BOWL	PUBLICATION	COMMENTS
Isa. 40.31	Isa. 40.31	MS 2053/140	JBA 98	❖ Exod. 3.15, Isa. 40.31
וק[י] יהוה [י]לפ[ו]ן כה ולהי אלא בל חשים ישהי אלה יגעו ולא יע[פו]	יְקַוֵּי יְהוָה וּפַלְמִין חֵיל יְקַוֵּי יִסְקוּן מַשִּׁירְיָן אֱלַהִי יִרְהָטוּן וְלָא יִלְאוּן			Other quotations: ❖ Isa. 60.11 ↔ Gen. 27.28
Isa. 40.31	Isa. 40.31	MS 2053/215	JBA 101	❖ Exod. 3.15, Isa. 40.31
יקוי יהוה [...]	יְקַוֵּי יְהוָה וּפַלְמִין חֵיל יְקַוֵּי יִסְקוּן מַשִּׁירְיָן אֱלַהִי יִרְהָטוּן וְלָא יִלְאוּן			Other quotations: ❖ Isa. 60.11 ↔ Gen. 27.28 The writing is extremely faded
Isa. 40.31	Isa. 40.31	M 142	Corpus: 93-94	Other quotations: ❖ Num. 32.22, Num. 14.9
וקוי יהוה יחלפו כ[ח] י אבן כנשרא נשרי אלה יגעו ולא ייעפו	יְקַוֵּי יְהוָה וּפַלְמִין חֵיל יְקַוֵּי יִסְקוּן מַשִּׁירְיָן אֱלַהִי יִרְהָטוּן וְלָא יִלְאוּן			
Isa. 40.31	Isa. 40.31	MS 2053/257	Shaked 2011: 210	Partial publication of bowl text
וקוי ייי יחלפו כה יקוי יסקון מ[שרין] אלה ויגי ולא [ייעפו]	יְקַוֵּי יְהוָה וּפַלְמִין חֵיל יְקַוֵּי יִסְקוּן מַשִּׁירְיָן אֱלַהִי יִרְהָטוּן וְלָא יִלְאוּן			

QUOTATION	MT/TARGUM	BOWL	PUBLICATION	COMMENTS
Isa. 40.31	Isa. 40.31	Aaron E	Geller 1986: 114	
[וקוי] הוהי יפילחו הכ ויעגיי אלו וצרי ופעי אלו וכלי	וקוי הוהי יפילחו הכ ויעגיי אלו וצרי ופעי אלו וכלי ויעגיי אלו			
Isa. 44.25	Isa. 44.25	BM 91735	CAMIB 35	Other quotations: Num. 10.35
מ(ע)פר םידב תותא רפמ ללוהי םימסקו רוחא םימכח בישמ םתעדו לכסי	מפר םידב תותא רפמ ללוהי םימסקו רוחא םימכח בישמ םתעדו לכסי			
Isa. 44.25	Isa. 44.25	BM 91765	Isbell 66 = CAMIB 26	✧ Song 3.7, Num. 6.24-26, Isa. 44.25
םימוקיו ןמ היב תותא רפמ ללוהי םימסקו רוחא םימכח בישמ םתעדו לכסי	מפר םידב תותא רפמ ללוהי םימסקו רוחא םימכח בישמ םתעדו לכסי			

QUOTATION	MT/TARGUM	BOWL	PUBLICATION	COMMENTS
Isa. 45.2 אני לפניך אהלך והדורים אושר דלתות נחושה אשבר ובריחי ברזל אגדע	Isa. 45.2 אֲנִי לְפָנֶיךָ אֵלֵךְ וַהֲדוּרִים אושר [אֲיַשֵּׁר] דַּלְתוֹת נְחוּשָׁה אֲשַׁבֵּר וּבְרִיחֵי בַרְזֶל אֲגַדֵּעַ	M 155	Corpus: 111	'By means of Gabriel and Michael and Raphael who shatter "copper doors" and cut "iron bars," may they shatter and cut off the evil spirit (afflicting the beneficiary)'
Isa. 50.11 הן כלכם קדחי אש מזרי זיקות לכו באור אשכם ובזיקות בערתם מידי היתה זאת לכם למעצבה תשכבון	Isa. 50.11 הֵן כֻּלְּכֶם קֹדְחֵי אֵשׁ מְאַזְּרֵי זִיקוֹת לְכוּ בְּאוּר אֶשְׁכֶם וּבְזִיקוֹת בִּעַרְתֶּם מִיָּדִי הָיְתָה־זֹּאת לָכֶם לְמַעֲצֵבָה תִּשְׁכָּבוּן	M 164	Levene 2007	✣ Isa. 50.11, Ps. 116.6, Ps. 91.11 Other quotations: Dan. 7.11, Exod. 23.21 The bowl text also quotes m. Šebu. 4.13, and thus includes several other partial biblical quotations in the form of divine epithets

QUOTATION	MT/TARGUM	BOWL	PUBLICATION	COMMENTS
Isa. 50.11	Isa. 50.11	MS 1927/14	JBA 113	❖ Isa. 50.11, Ps. 125.2
הן כלכם קדחי אש [קודי זקות] מכאש אור [לכה] באור אשכם וביקות בערתם מידי היתה זאת לכם למעצבה תשכבון	הָ֤ן כֻּלְּכֶם֙ קֹ֣דְחֵי אֵ֔שׁ מְאַזְּרֵ֖י זִיקֹ֑ות לְכ֣וּ ׀ בְּא֣וּר אֶשְׁכֶ֗ם וּבְזִיקֹות֙ בִּֽעַרְתֶּ֔ם מִיָּדִי֙ הָיְתָה־זֹּ֣את לָכֶ֔ם לְמַעֲצֵבָ֖ה תִּשְׁכָּבֽוּן			
Isa. 50.11	Isa. 50.11	MS 2053/45	JBA 114	
[הן] אש [הן קו]דחי אש מ[ז]רי קדות מכאש אור לכה באור אשכם וביקות בערתם מידי היתה זאת לכם למעצבה [ת]שכבון[ו]	הָ֤ן כֻּלְּכֶם֙ קֹ֣דְחֵי אֵ֔שׁ מְאַזְּרֵ֖י זִיקֹ֑ות לְכ֣וּ ׀ בְּא֣וּר אֶשְׁכֶ֗ם וּבְזִיקֹות֙ בִּֽעַרְתֶּ֔ם מִיָּדִי֙ הָיְתָה־זֹּ֣את לָכֶ֔ם לְמַעֲצֵבָ֖ה תִּשְׁכָּבֽוּן			
Isa. 50.11	Isa. 50.11	IM 56544	ZHS 2a	❖ Isa. 50.11, Exod. 15.12
בנבערה אצבעהון	הָ֤ן כֻּלְּכֶם֙ קֹ֣דְחֵי אֵ֔שׁ מְאַזְּרֵ֖י זִיקֹ֑ות לְכ֣וּ ׀ בְּא֣וּר אֶשְׁכֶ֗ם וּבְזִיקֹות֙ בִּֽעַרְתֶּ֔ם מִיָּדִי֙ הָיְתָה־זֹּ֣את לָכֶ֔ם לְמַעֲצֵבָ֖ה תִּשְׁכָּבֽוּן			An allusive bowl text, whose various citations are invoked as names of power: בנבערה
Isa. 51.14	Isa. 51.14	Matenadaran MS 132	Abousamra 2019	❖ Zech. 3.2, Isa. 51.14
מהר צעה להפתה ולא ימות לשחת ולא יחסר לחמו	מִהַ֥ר צֹעֶ֖ה לְהִפָּתֵ֑חַ וְלֹא־יָמ֣וּת לַשַּׁ֔חַת וְלֹ֥א יֶחְסַ֖ר לַחְמֹֽו			

P

QUOTATION	MT/TARGUM	BOWL	PUBLICATION	COMMENTS
P Isa. 51.15 = Jer 31.34 הוה צבאות שמו ברגע הים ויהמו גליו יהוה אלהיך רגע	Isa. 51.15 וְאָנֹכִי יְהוָה אֱלֹהֶיךָ רֹגַע הַיָּם וַיֶּהֱמוּ גַּלָּיו יְהוָה צְבָאוֹת שְׁמוֹ	—	Shaked 2015: 109-110	Other quotations: Ps. 115.1-2
Isa. 60.6 שפעת גמלים תכסך בכרי מדין ועיפה כלם משבא יבאו זהב ולבונה ישאו ותהלות יהוה יבשרו	Isa. 60.6 שִׁפְעַת גְּמַלִּים תְּכַסֵּךְ בִּכְרֵי מִדְיָן וְעֵיפָה כֻּלָּם מִשְּׁבָא יָבֹאוּ זָהָב וּלְבוֹנָה יִשָּׂאוּ וּתְהִלֹּת יְהוָה יְבַשֵּׂרוּ	SD 34	Levene/ Bhayro 2005/2006	For success in business ✣ Isa. 60.11, Isa. 60.6, Isa. 60.8
Isa. 60.8 מי אלה כעב תעופינה וכיונים אל ארבתיהם	Isa. 60.8 מִי־אֵלֶּה כָּעָב תְּעוּפֶינָה וְכַיּוֹנִים אֶל־אֲרֻבֹּתֵיהֶם	SD 34	Levene/ Bhayro 2005/2006	For success in business ✣ Isa. 60.11, Isa. 60.6, Isa. 60.8

	QUOTATION	MT/TARGUM	BOWL	PUBLICATION	COMMENTS
	Isa. 60.11	Isa. 60.11	SD 34	Levene/Bhayro 2005/2006	For success in business ✥ Isa. 60.11, Isa. 60.6, Isa. 60.8
C P	Isa. 60.11 ⇄ Gen. 27.28	Isa. 60.11	MS 1911/1	JBA 65	'For (the) livelihood' (לחיותה) of the beneficiary ✥ Isa. 60.11 ↔ Gen. 27.28 Other quotations: ✥ Exod. 3.15, Isa. 40.31 CF: שומרך
C	Isa. 60.11 ⇄ Gen. 27.28	Isa. 60.11	MS 2053/56	JBA 67	✥ Isa. 60.11 ↔ Gen. 27.28 Other quotations: ✥ Exod. 3.15, Isa. 40.31; ✥ Ps. 121.7-8, Zech. 3.2 CF: שומרך

	QUOTATION	MT/TARGUM	BOWL	PUBLICATION	COMMENTS
C	Isa. 60.11 ⇄ Gen. 27.28	Isa. 60.11	MS 2053/69	JBA 95	✤ Isa. 60.11 ↔ Gen. 27.28
P	ויתן [הם] ייבה הטל ושעיר וטמרה לילה ולא יטגרו לבנה אלא יום הן גוים מהנבאה	ופתחו שעריך תמיד יומם ולילה לא יסגרו להביא אליך חיל גוים ומלכיהם נהוגים			Other quotations: ✤ Exod. 3.15, Isa. 40.31 CF: שאבכר
C	Isa. 60.11 ⇄ Gen. 27.28	Isa. 60.11	MS 2053/140	JBA 98	✤ Isa. 60.11 ↔ Gen. 27.28
P	ויתן [ו]ם ייבה הטל ושעיר וטמרה לילה ולא יטגרו להביא אליך חיל גוים מהנבאה	ופתחו שעריך תמיד יומם ולילה לא יסגרו להביא אליך חיל גוים ומלכיהם נהוגים			Other quotations: ✤ Exod. 3.15, Isa. 40.31 CF: שאבכר
C	Isa. 60.11 ⇄ Gen. 27.28	Isa. 60.11	MS 2053/215	JBA 101	✤ Isa. 60.11 ↔ Gen. 27.28
P	[...] ולילה [יום ...] ופתח[ו	ופתחו שעריך תמיד יומם ולילה לא יסגרו להביא אליך חיל גוים ומלכיהם נהוגים			Other quotations: ✤ Exod. 3.15, Isa. 40.31 CF: שאבכר The writing is extremely faded

QUOTATION	MT/TARGUM	BOWL	PUBLICATION	COMMENTS
א Jer. 2.1 = Ezek. 21.23 ס היה דבר יהוה אלי לאמר T הוה פתגם נבואה מן קדם יהוה עמי לאמר (Tg. Neb.)	Jer. 2.1 ויהי דבר יהוה אלי לאמר (MT)	OI A33965 10N-16	Kaufman 1973	✢ Ezek. 21.21-22, Jer. 2.2 (T), Jer. 2.3, Jer. 2.1 (T)
א Jer. 2.2 ס הלך וקראת באזני ירושלם לאמר כה אמר יהוה זכרתי לך חסד נעוריך אהבת כלולתיך לכתך אחרי במדבר בארץ לא זרועה [אחר] T איזיל ותתנבי קדם עמא דבירושלם למימר כדנן אמר יי דכירנא לכון טבות יומי קדמיתא חיבת אבהתכון עממיא אתרעותי בכון לאפקותכון פריקין מארע מצרים ודברית יתכון במדברא בארע צדיא ושוממא (Tg. Neb.)	Jer. 2.2 הלך וקראת באזני ירושלם לאמר כה אמר יהוה זכרתי לך חסד נעוריך אהבת כלולתיך לכתך אחרי במדבר בארץ לא זרועה (MT)	OI A33965 10N-16	Kaufman 1973	✢ Ezek. 21.21-22, Jer. 2.2 (T), Jer. 2.3, Jer. 2.1 (T)

QUOTATION	MT/TARGUM	BOWL	PUBLICATION	COMMENTS
אנבראה שוין בלה לא הווה ידעין במרומא אבלעא				
N Jer. 2.3 S	Jer. 2.3 קֹדֶשׁ יִשְׂרָאֵל לַיהוָה רֵאשִׁית תְּבוּאָתֹה כָּל־אֹכְלָיו יֶאְשָׁמוּ רָעָה תָּבֹא אֲלֵיהֶם נְאֻם־יְהוָה	OI A33965 10N-16	Kaufman 1973	✣ Ezek. 21.21-22, Jer. 2.2 (T), Jer. 2.3, Jer. 2.1 (T)
N Jer. 5.22 P	Jer. 5.22 הַאוֹתִי לֹא־תִירָאוּ נְאֻם־יְהוָה אִם מִפָּנַי לֹא תָחִילוּ אֲשֶׁר־שַׂמְתִּי חוֹל גְּבוּל לַיָּם חָק־עוֹלָם וְלֹא יַעַבְרֶנְהוּ וַיִּתְגָּעֲשׁוּ וְלֹא יוּכָלוּ וְהָמוּ גַלָּיו וְלֹא יַעַבְרֻנְהוּ	—	Ford/Ten-Ami 2012	

QUOTATION	MT/TARGUM	BOWL	PUBLICATION	COMMENTS
Jer. 8.4 = Amos 8.14 ↔ Lev. 26.37	Jer. 8.4 הכה (אל) ונפל(ו) אלו ולא ישבו אמרה מנולבה אלן קומה הזה אותה שוב	הכה יקום הב מפילא קימתא אלן ישוב אם ומארי אלן ולמיתב שוב	—	AMB 9	For cursing a named individual **CF:** הקמחא קומה עלוה מארא הוב Other quotations: ✢ Ps. 69.24, Ps. 69.26, Exod. 22.23, Deut. 28.22, Deut. 28.35, Deut. 28.28, Lev. 26.29; ✢ Mic. 7.16-17, Deut. 29.19; [≅ Jer. 8.4 = Amos 8.14 ↔ Lev. 26.37]
Jer. 31.34 = Isa. 51.15	Jer. 31.34 הוה ולא יסדו עוד איש את רעהו ואיש את אחיו	יאלף ילפון עוד הלא יסדו עוד איש את רעהו ואיש את אחיו לאמר דעו את יהוה כי כולם ידעו אותי למקטנם ועד גדולם נאם יהוה	—	Shaked 2015: 109-110	**CF:** הכהנא Other quotations: Ps. 115.1-2

	QUOTATION	MT/TARGUM		BOWL	PUBLICATION	COMMENTS
א C	Ezek. 1.5 ↔ Ezek. 1.27 והנה היה הזה מראת דמות אדם הנה היה לו דמות ארבע	Ezek. 1.5 וּמִתּוֹכָהּ דְּמוּת אַרְבַּע חַיּוֹת וְזֶה מַרְאֵיהֶן דְּמוּת אָדָם לָהֵנָּה		M 1	Shaked 1995: 207	Other quotations: Deut. 32.3; ✜ Ezek. 1.27 ↔ Ezek. 1.5; Isa. 6.3
א C	Ezek. 1.27 ↔ Ezek. 1.5 וארבע הזה הזה לו דמות ארבע הנה היה הזה מראת דמות אדם	Ezek. 1.27 וָאֵרֶא כְּעֵין חַשְׁמַל כְּמַרְאֵה־אֵשׁ בֵּית־לָהּ סָבִיב מִמַּרְאֵה מָתְנָיו וּלְמָעְלָה וּמִמַּרְאֵה מָתְנָיו וּלְמַטָּה רָאִיתִי כְּמַרְאֵה־אֵשׁ וְנֹגַהּ לוֹ סָבִיב		M 1	Shaked 1995: 207	Other quotations: Deut. 32.3; ✜ Ezek. 1.27 ↔ Ezek. 1.5; Isa. 6.3
א S ϕ	Ezek. 21.21-22 התאחדי הימיני השמאילי באשר פניך מעדות וגם אני אכה כפי אל כפי והניחתי חמתי אני יהוה דברתי	Ezek. 21.21-22 הִתְאַחֲדִי הֵימִנִי הַשְׂמִילִי אָנָה פָּנַיִךְ מֻעָדוֹת וְגַם־אֲנִי אַכֶּה כַפִּי אֶל־כַּפִּי וַהֲנִחֹתִי חֲמָתִי אֲנִי יְהוָה דִּבַּרְתִּי		OI A33965 10N-16	Kaufman 1973	✜ Ezek. 21.21-22, Jer. 2.2 (T), Jer. 2.3, Jer. 2.1 (T)

Catalogue 109

	QUOTATION	MT/TARGUM	BOWL	PUBLICATION	COMMENTS
א	Ezek. 32.27 ויהיו לא ישכבו את גבורים נפלים מערלים אשר ירדו שאול בכלי מלחמתם ויתנו את חרבותם תחת ראשיהם ותהי עונתם על עצמותם כי חתית גבורים בארץ חיים	Ezek. 32.27 וְלֹא יִשְׁכְּבוּ אֶת־גִּבּוֹרִים נֹפְלִים מֵעֲרֵלִים אֲשֶׁר יָרְדוּ־ שְׁאוֹל בִּכְלֵי־מִלְחַמְתָּם וַיִּתְּנוּ אֶת־חַרְבוֹתָם תַּחַת רָאשֵׁיהֶם וַתְּהִי עֲוֺנֹתָם עַל־ עַצְמוֹתָם כִּי־חִתִּית גִּבּוֹרִים בְּאֶרֶץ חַיִּים	M 6	Shaked 1995: 211-213	✣ Num. 9.23, Zech. 3.2, Ezek. 32.27, Ps. 91.11
א p	Ezek. 32.27 ותהי עונותם על עצמותם כי חתית גבורים בארץ ח[יים] [...]	Ezek. 32.27 וְלֹא יִשְׁכְּבוּ אֶת־גִּבּוֹרִים נֹפְלִים מֵעֲרֵלִים אֲשֶׁר יָרְדוּ־ שְׁאוֹל בִּכְלֵי־מִלְחַמְתָּם וַיִּתְּנוּ אֶת־חַרְבוֹתָם תַּחַת רָאשֵׁיהֶם וַתְּהִי עֲוֺנֹתָם עַל־ עַצְמוֹתָם כִּי־חִתִּית גִּבּוֹרִים בְּאֶרֶץ חַיִּים	Einhorn 4	MSF 22	✣ Num. 9.23, Ezek. 32.27 The writing is extremely faded The quotation appears to comprise only Ezek. 32.27b

QUOTATION	MT/TARGUM	BOWL	PUBLICATION	COMMENTS
Hos. 2.2-4 ריבו באמכם ריבו כי לא אשה [הם] ואנכי לא אישה[ה] והסר זנוניה מפניה ונאפופיה מבין שדיה פן אפשיטנ[ה] ערמה והצגתיה כיום הולדה ושמתיה כמדבר ושתה כארץ ציה והמיתיה בצמא ואת בניה לא ארחם כי בני זנו[ני] המה	Hos. 2.2-4 וְאִמְרוּ לַאֲחֵיכֶם עַמִּי וְלַאֲחוֹתֵיכֶם רֻחָמָה רִיבוּ בְאִמְּכֶם רִיבוּ כִּי הִיא לֹא אִשְׁתִּי וְאָנֹכִי לֹא אִישָׁהּ וְתָסֵר זְנוּנֶיהָ מִפָּנֶיה וְנַאֲפוּפֶיהָ מִבֵּין שָׁדֶיהָ פֶּן אַפְשִׁיטֶנָּה עֲרֻמָּה וְהִצַּגְתִּיהָ כְּיוֹם הִוָּלְדָהּ וְשַׂמְתִּיהָ כַמִּדְבָּר וְשַׁתִּהָ כְּאֶרֶץ צִיָּה וַהֲמִתִּיהָ בַּצָּמָא וְאֶת בָּנֶיהָ לֹא אֲרַחֵם כִּי בְנֵי זְנוּנִים הֵמָּה	CBS 3997	AIT 26 = Shaked 1999: 194	Other quotations: ✤ Deut. 6.4, Num. 9.23, Zech. 3.2 The quotation is partially effaced. Montgomery (1913, 210) "reproduced … the evident characters" but did not recognise Hos. 2.2-4 here. Cf. Rossell (1953, 3, 87)

QUOTATION	MT/TARGUM	BOWL	PUBLICATION	COMMENTS
Amos 8.14 = Jer. 8.4 ↔ Lev. 26.37	Amos 8.14	—	AMB 9	For cursing a named individual
הנה (אל) ומו(ק)י אלו ולבר אחו אלו ארלבמה אמרה מחטאת נחוטא	וישתע ונפאצא בשבעבדו ירי יון די אלוהא יד ורנא יום ומאקר אלו ובמו נפש ראש			**CF:** הנה הקם נאקר לילע קמרה Other quotations: ✣ Ps. 69.24, Ps. 69.26, Exod. 22.23, Deut. 28.22, Deut. 28.35, Deut. 28.28, Lev. 26.29; ✣ Mic. 7.16-17, Deut. 29.19; [≅ Jer. 8.4 = Amos 8.14 ↔ Lev. 26.37]
Mic. 7.16-17	Mic. 7.16-17	—	AMB 9	See above
לבכה ושהוה מוה ואהיו בה [על] די ומו[ש׳ מהי]נו והלי נושחה מרוזאו פדאר ידוזב שרוה [נפש] מחחהאפמרו ו[ורו]	מהיוגא לבם ושזה מוה אראי ומושע: וחלק נשותהם מרגזונה יראו על פני אמרים מחגבלל מרחהאמרוחה לל אחר ולא ירא ולא יבא את ראש ועם:			

QUOTATION	MT/TARGUM	BOWL	PUBLICATION	COMMENTS
Zech. 3.2 ויאמר יהוה אל השטן יגער יהוה בך השטן ויגער יהוה בך הבחר בירושלים הלוא זה אוד מצל מאש	Zech. 3.2 וַיֹּאמֶר יְהוָה אֶל־הַשָּׂטָן יִגְעַר יְהוָה בְּךָ הַשָּׂטָן וְיִגְעַר יְהוָה בְּךָ הַבֹּחֵר בִּירוּשָׁלָ͏ִם הֲלוֹא זֶה אוּד מֻצָּל מֵאֵשׁ	MFL 10895	Bhayro 2017	For fertility and success in childbirth Other quotations: Gen. 30.22
Zech. 3.2 ויאמר יהוה אל השטן יגער יהוה בך השטן ויגער יהוה בך הבחר בירושלים הלוא זה אוד מצל מאש	Zech. 3.2 וַיֹּאמֶר יְהוָה אֶל־הַשָּׂטָן יִגְעַר יְהוָה בְּךָ הַשָּׂטָן וְיִגְעַר יְהוָה בְּךָ הַבֹּחֵר בִּירוּשָׁלָ͏ִם הֲלוֹא זֶה אוּד מֻצָּל מֵאֵשׁ	—	Abousamra 2020	
Zech. 3.2 יגער השטן אל יהוה יהוה בך השטן ויגער יהוה בך הבחר בירושלים הלוא זה אוד מצל מאש	Zech. 3.2 וַיֹּאמֶר יְהוָה אֶל־הַשָּׂטָן יִגְעַר יְהוָה בְּךָ הַשָּׂטָן וְיִגְעַר יְהוָה בְּךָ הַבֹּחֵר בִּירוּשָׁלָ͏ִם הֲלוֹא זֶה אוּד מֻצָּל מֵאֵשׁ	S-448	SHM 6	

	QUOTATION	MT/TARGUM	BOWL	PUBLICATION	COMMENTS
א	Zech. 3.2 יגער [אל יה]ו[ה] [את]ן יגער יהוה בך השטן יגער יהוה בך הבוחר בירושלים מ[ו]ד את לה מאש	Zech. 3.2 וַיֹּאמֶר יְהוָה אֶל הַשָּׂטָן יִגְעַר יְהוָה בְּךָ הַשָּׂטָן וְיִגְעַר יְהוָה בְּךָ הַבֹּחֵר בִּירוּשָׁלִָם הֲלוֹא זֶה אוּד מֻצָּל מֵאֵשׁ	MS 2053/7	Bohak 2012: 47	Repeated at two different points in the bowl Other quotations: Num. 10.35-36
	[יגר] יגער אל יהוה יהוה מאר[ן]ה יגער יהוה בך [שטן]ה יגער יהוה בך הבחר בירושלים הלוא זה אוד מצל מאש				
א	Zech. 3.2 יגער אל [יה]ו[ה] [יאמר] [יגר] יגער יהוה בך [שטן] ב[ירושלים] [הבחר] בך יהוה מאש מצל אוד זה הלוא	Zech. 3.2 וַיֹּאמֶר יְהוָה אֶל הַשָּׂטָן יִגְעַר יְהוָה בְּךָ הַשָּׂטָן וְיִגְעַר יְהוָה בְּךָ הַבֹּחֵר בִּירוּשָׁלִָם הֲלוֹא זֶה אוּד מֻצָּל מֵאֵשׁ	MS 2053/13	Shaked 2011: 209	Other quotations: Num. 6.24-26

QUOTATION	MT/TARGUM	BOWL	PUBLICATION	COMMENTS
Zech. 3.2 ויאמר יהוה {ס} [ה]סטן {נ} יגער יהוה בך הסטן ויגער יהוה בך הבחר בירושלים הלוא זה אוד מצל מאש	Zech. 3.2 וַיֹּאמֶר יְהוָה אֶל־הַשָּׂטָן יִגְעַר יְהוָה בְּךָ הַשָּׂטָן וְיִגְעַר יְהוָה בְּךָ הַבֹּחֵר בִּירוּשָׁלִָם הֲלוֹא זֶה אוּד מֻצָּל מֵאֵשׁ	MS 2053/56	JBA 67	✣ Ps. 121.7-8, Zech. 3.2 Other quotations: ✣ Exod. 3.15, Isa. 40.31; ✣ Isa. 60.11 ↔ Gen. 27.28 (T)
Zech. 3.2 ויאמר יהוה אל הסטן יגער יהוה בך הסטן ויגער יהוה בך הבוחר בירושלים הלוא זה אוד מצל מאש	Zech. 3.2 וַיֹּאמֶר יְהוָה אֶל־הַשָּׂטָן יִגְעַר יְהוָה בְּךָ הַשָּׂטָן וְיִגְעַר יְהוָה בְּךָ הַבֹּחֵר בִּירוּשָׁלִָם הֲלוֹא זֶה אוּד מֻצָּל מֵאֵשׁ	MS 2053/196	JBA 103	✣ Num. 9.23, Zech. 3.2 Other quotations: ✣ Ps. 55.8, Ps. 91.7
Zech. 3.2 ויאמ[ר] יהוה אל הסט[ן] יגע[ר] יהוה בך הסטן ב[ה]והי[ה] ויגער יהוה ב[י]רוש[לי]ם הלוא זה אוד מצל מאש	Zech. 3.2 וַיֹּאמֶר יְהוָה אֶל־הַשָּׂטָן יִגְעַר יְהוָה בְּךָ הַשָּׂטָן וְיִגְעַר יְהוָה בְּךָ הַבֹּחֵר בִּירוּשָׁלִָם הֲלוֹא זֶה אוּד מֻצָּל מֵאֵשׁ	MS 2053/238	JBA 104	Written on the exterior of the bowl

Catalogue 115

	QUOTATION	MT/TARGUM	BOWL	PUBLICATION	COMMENTS
א	Zech. 3.2	Zech. 3.2	MS 2053/218	JBA 108	❖ Zech. 3.2, Num. 12.13
	ויאמר יהוה [א]ל השטן יגער יהוה בך השטן [...] יהוה בך הבחר בירושלם אל נא קרבא [ש]	וַיֹּאמֶר יְהוָה אֶל הַשָּׂטָן יִגְעַר יְהוָה בְּךָ הַשָּׂטָן וְיִגְעַר יְהוָה בְּךָ הַבֹּחֵר בִּירוּשָׁלִָם הֲלוֹא זֶה אוּד מֻצָּל מֵאֵשׁ			
א	Zech. 3.2	Zech. 3.2	MS 2053/230	JBA 109	❖ Zech. 3.2, Ps. 55.9
	יגר יהוה אל השטן ויגר יהוה בך השטן ויגר יהוה בך הבוחר בירושלים הלוא זה אוד מצל מאש אחישה מפלט לי	וַיֹּאמֶר יְהוָה אֶל הַשָּׂטָן יִגְעַר יְהוָה בְּךָ הַשָּׂטָן וְיִגְעַר יְהוָה בְּךָ הַבֹּחֵר בִּירוּשָׁלִָם הֲלוֹא זֶה אוּד מֻצָּל מֵאֵשׁ			

	QUOTATION	MT/TARGUM	BOWL	PUBLICATION	COMMENTS
א S	Zech. 3.2 ויאמר יהוה אל השטן יגער יהוה בך השטן ויגער יהוה בך הבחר בירושלים הלוא זה אוד מצל מאש	Zech. 3.2 וַיֹּאמֶר יְהוָה אֶל הַשָּׂטָן יִגְעַר יְהוָה בְּךָ הַשָּׂטָן וְיִגְעַר יְהוָה בָּךְ הַבֹּחֵר בִּירוּשָׁלִָם הֲלוֹא זֶה אוּד מֻצָּל מֵאֵשׁ	IM 141803	Faraj 2010: 206-207	❖ Exod. 15.14-17 (Exod. 15.14 x2), Zech. 3.2, Prov. 30.17 The text of the bowl is divided into four sections arranged around a drawing of a demonic figure.
א	Zech. 3.2 ויאמר יהוה אל השטן יגער יהוה בך ה[סט]ן אכב ה יהוה ם[שו]ירושלים היחנה אה זה מצל {את} זה את ה(לו) אש מ(אש)	Zech. 3.2 וַיֹּאמֶר יְהוָה אֶל הַשָּׂטָן יִגְעַר יְהוָה בְּךָ הַשָּׂטָן וְיִגְעַר יְהוָה בָּךְ הַבֹּחֵר בִּירוּשָׁלִָם הֲלוֹא זֶה אוּד מֻצָּל מֵאֵשׁ	JHMB 242/1	AMB 11	❖ Zech. 3.2, Deut. 6.4 ⇄ Ps. 91.1
א	Zech. 3.2 ויאמר יהוה אל השטן יגער יהוה בך השטן ויגער יהוה בך הבחר בירושלים הלוא זה אוד מצל מאש	Zech. 3.2 וַיֹּאמֶר יְהוָה אֶל הַשָּׂטָן יִגְעַר יְהוָה בְּךָ הַשָּׂטָן וְיִגְעַר יְהוָה בָּךְ הַבֹּחֵר בִּירוּשָׁלִָם הֲלוֹא זֶה אוּד מֻצָּל מֵאֵשׁ	M 6	Shaked 1995: 211-213	❖ Num. 9.23, Zech. 3.2, Ezek. 32.27, Ps. 91.11

QUOTATION	MT/TARGUM	BOWL	PUBLICATION	COMMENTS
Zech. 3.2 ויאמר יהוה אל השטן יגער יהוה בך השטן ויגער יהוה בך הבחר בירושלים הלוא זה אוד מצל מאש)	Zech. 3.2 וַיֹּאמֶר יְהוָה אֶל-הַשָּׂטָן יִגְעַר יְהוָה בְּךָ הַשָּׂטָן וְיִגְעַר יְהוָה בְּךָ הַבֹּחֵר בִּירוּשָׁלִָם הֲלוֹא זֶה אוּד מֻצָּל מֵאֵשׁ	M 59	Corpus: 35-37	Written on the exterior of the bowl
Zech. 3.2 ויאמר יהוה אל השטן יגער יהוה בך השטן ויגער יהוה בך הבהר בירושלים הלוא זה אוד מצל מאש	Zech. 3.2 וַיֹּאמֶר יְהוָה אֶל-הַשָּׂטָן יִגְעַר יְהוָה בְּךָ הַשָּׂטָן וְיִגְעַר יְהוָה בְּךָ הַבֹּחֵר בִּירוּשָׁלִָם הֲלוֹא זֶה אוּד מֻצָּל מֵאֵשׁ	M 108	Corpus: 71	✢ Ps. 106.47 ⇄ 1 Chron. 16.35, Zech. 3.2, Ps. 89.53, Ps. 106.48, Ps. 72.18-19, Ps. 104.31 Cf. *Seder ʿAmram: ʿArvit* Invoked as name of power: בשום The bowl text consists almost solely of biblical verses

QUOTATION	MT/TARGUM	BOWL	PUBLICATION	COMMENTS
ℵ Zech. 3.2 וַיֹּאמֶר יְהוָה אֶל הַשָּׂטָן יִגְעַר יְהוָה בְּךָ הַשָּׂטָן וְיִגְעַר יְהוָה בָּךְ <בּ>הַבֹּחֵר בִּירוּשָׁלָיִם הֲלוֹא זֶה אוּד מֻצָּל מֵאֵשׁ	Zech. 3.2 וַיֹּאמֶר יְהוָה אֶל הַשָּׂטָן יִגְעַר יְהוָה בְּךָ הַשָּׂטָן וְיִגְעַר יְהוָה בְּךָ הַבֹּחֵר בִּירוּשָׁלָיִם הֲלוֹא זֶה אוּד מֻצָּל מֵאֵשׁ	Matenadaran MS 132	Abousamra 2019	✣ Zech. 3.2, Isa. 51.14
ℵ Zech. 3.2 ויאמר יהוה אל השטן יגער יהוה בך השטן ויגער יהוה בך אז לא הבחר בירושלים הלוא זה אוד מצל מאש	Zech. 3.2 וַיֹּאמֶר יְהוָה אֶל הַשָּׂטָן יִגְעַר יְהוָה בְּךָ הַשָּׂטָן וְיִגְעַר יְהוָה בְּךָ הַבֹּחֵר בִּירוּשָׁלָיִם הֲלוֹא זֶה אוּד מֻצָּל מֵאֵשׁ	BM 139524	Geller 1980: 54 = CAMIB 23	
ℵ Zech. 3.2 ו[יאמ]ר יה[וה] אל ה[שט]ן יגער [יה]וה ב[ך] ויגער יהוה בך ויהבחר בירושלים הל[וא] זה אוד מ[צל] א[ש]	Zech. 3.2 וַיֹּאמֶר יְהוָה אֶל הַשָּׂטָן יִגְעַר יְהוָה בְּךָ הַשָּׂטָן וְיִגְעַר יְהוָה בְּךָ הַבֹּחֵר בִּירוּשָׁלָיִם הֲלוֹא זֶה אוּד מֻצָּל מֵאֵשׁ	HS 3022	Ford/Morgenstern 2020: 68-69	✣ Num. 11.2, Num. 9.23, Num. 12.13, Zech. 3.2

	QUOTATION	MT/TARGUM	BOWL	PUBLICATION	COMMENTS
א	Zech. 3.2 ויאמר ייי אל השטן יגער ייי בך השטן ויגער ייי בך הבחר בירושלים הלו[א] זה אוד מצל מאש	Zech. 3.2 וַיֹּ֨אמֶר יְהוָ֜ה אֶל־הַשָּׂטָ֗ן יִגְעַ֨ר יְהוָ֤ה בְּךָ֙ הַשָּׂטָ֔ן וְיִגְעַ֤ר יְהוָה֙ בְּךָ֔ הַבֹּחֵ֖ר בִּירוּשָׁלִָ֑ם הֲל֧וֹא זֶ֦ה א֖וּד מֻצָּ֥ל מֵאֵֽשׁ	T 15608	Misgav 2018	
א	Zech. 3.2 יגער יהוה בך [ו]יגער יהוה בך הבחר [בה] זה אוד מצל מאש	Zech. 3.2 יִגְעַ֨ר יְהוָ֤ה בְּךָ֙ הַשָּׂטָ֔ן וְיִגְעַ֤ר יְהוָה֙ בְּךָ֔ הַבֹּחֵ֖ר בִּירוּשָׁלִָ֑ם הֲל֧וֹא זֶ֦ה א֖וּד מֻצָּ֥ל מֵאֵֽשׁ	T 27987	Misgav 2018	Other quotations: Deut. 6.4
א	Zech. 3.2 [... יהוה אל השטן] ויאמר [... בירושלים]	Zech. 3.2 וַיֹּ֨אמֶר יְהוָ֜ה אֶל־הַשָּׂטָ֗ן יִגְעַ֨ר יְהוָ֤ה בְּךָ֙ הַשָּׂטָ֔ן וְיִגְעַ֤ר יְהוָה֙ בְּךָ֔ הַבֹּחֵ֖ר בִּירוּשָׁלִָ֑ם הֲל֧וֹא זֶ֦ה א֖וּד מֻצָּ֥ל מֵאֵֽשׁ	T 28001	Misgav 2018	Extremely faded text, written in radial lines

QUOTATION	MT/TARGUM	BOWL	PUBLICATION	COMMENTS
Zech. 3.2 ויאמר יהוה אל הסטן {יאמר} יגער יהוה בך {הסטן} יגער יהוה {בך} בך יהוה יהוה אשר בחר בירושלים ה[ז]ה {מאש} [זה]}	Zech. 3.2 וַיֹּאמֶר יְהוָה אֶל הַשָּׂטָן יִגְעַר יְהוָה בְּךָ הַשָּׂטָן וְיִגְעַר יְהוָה בְּךָ הַבֹּחֵר בִּירוּשָׁלִָם הֲלוֹא זֶה אוּד מֻצָּל מֵאֵשׁ	Louvre AO 2099	Isbell 42	
Zech. 3.2 יגער יהוה בך הסטן ויגער יהוה בך יהוה הסטן בך יהוה אשר בחר בירושלים והנה [מאש]	Zech. 3.2 וַיֹּאמֶר יְהוָה אֶל הַשָּׂטָן יִגְעַר יְהוָה בְּךָ הַשָּׂטָן וְיִגְעַר יְהוָה בְּךָ הַבֹּחֵר בִּירוּשָׁלִָם הֲלוֹא זֶה אוּד מֻצָּל מֵאֵשׁ	CBS 2963	AIT 3	CF: שמאבד
Zech. 3.2 יגער יהוה בך הסטן ויגער יהוה בך יהוה הסטן בך יהוה אשר בחר בירושלים והנה אוד מצ[ו]ל מאש	Zech. 3.2 וַיֹּאמֶר יְהוָה אֶל הַשָּׂטָן יִגְעַר יְהוָה בְּךָ הַשָּׂטָן וְיִגְעַר יְהוָה בְּךָ הַבֹּחֵר בִּירוּשָׁלִָם הֲלוֹא זֶה אוּד מֻצָּל מֵאֵשׁ	CBS 2952	AIT 5	❖ Num. 9.23, Zech. 3.2

QUOTATION	MT/TARGUM	BOWL	PUBLICATION	COMMENTS
ℵ Zech. 3.2 ויאמר יהוה אל השטן יגער יהוה בך השטן יגער יהוה בך הבחר בירושלים הלוא זה אוד מֻצָּל מֵאֵשׁ	Zech. 3.2 וַיֹּאמֶר יְהוָה אֶל־הַשָּׂטָן יִגְעַר יְהוָה בְּךָ הַשָּׂטָן וְיִגְעַר יְהוָה בְּךָ הַבֹּחֵר בִּירוּשָׁלָ͏ִם הֲלוֹא זֶה אוּד מֻצָּל מֵאֵשׁ	CBS 2920	AIT 16	
ℵ Zech. 3.2 יהוה יגער יהוה בך השטן ויאמר יהוה בך הבחר בירושלים הלוא זה אוד מצל מאש	Zech. 3.2 וַיֹּאמֶר יְהוָה אֶל־הַשָּׂטָן יִגְעַר יְהוָה בְּךָ הַשָּׂטָן וְיִגְעַר יְהוָה בְּךָ הַבֹּחֵר בִּירוּשָׁלָ͏ִם הֲלוֹא זֶה אוּד מֻצָּל מֵאֵשׁ	CBS 3997	AIT 26 = Shaked 1999: 194	✣ Deut. 6.4, Num. 9.23, Zech. 3.2 Other quotations: Hos. 2.2-4
ℵ Zech. 3.2 יהוה יגער יה"ה בך [השטן ויאמר יהוה בך יג(ר) יה"ה בך הבחר בירושלי[ם] אוד זה אלהא מצל מא]ש	Zech. 3.2 וַיֹּאמֶר יְהוָה אֶל־הַשָּׂטָן יִגְעַר יְהוָה בְּךָ הַשָּׂטָן וְיִגְעַר יְהוָה בְּךָ הַבֹּחֵר בִּירוּשָׁלָ͏ִם הֲלוֹא זֶה אוּד מֻצָּל מֵאֵשׁ	Louvre AOD 361	Schwab 1891: 592	Other quotations: Deut. 6.4 ⇄ Ps. 91.1 Partial edition of the bowl text

QUOTATION	MT/TARGUM	BOWL	PUBLICATION	COMMENTS
ℵ Zech. 3.2 ויאמר יהוה אל השטן יגער יהוה בך השטן ויגער יהוה בך הבחר בירושלים הלוא זה אוד מצל מאש	Zech. 3.2 וַיֹּאמֶר יְהוָה אֶל־הַשָּׂטָן יִגְעַר יְהוָה בְּךָ הַשָּׂטָן וְיִגְעַר יְהוָה בְּךָ הַבֹּחֵר בִּירוּשָׁלִָם הֲלוֹא זֶה אוּד מֻצָּל מֵאֵשׁ	ZRL 48	Gordon 1978: 233	Other quotations: Deut. 6.4 ⇄ Ps. 91.1
ℵ Zech. 3.2 ויגער יהוה אל השטן יגער יהוה בך השטן ויגער יהוה בך הבחר בירושלים הלוא זה אלה מצל מאש	Zech. 3.2 וַיֹּאמֶר יְהוָה אֶל־הַשָּׂטָן יִגְעַר יְהוָה בְּךָ הַשָּׂטָן וְיִגְעַר יְהוָה בְּךָ הַבֹּחֵר בִּירוּשָׁלִָם הֲלוֹא זֶה אוּד מֻצָּל מֵאֵשׁ	Aaron B	Geller 1986: 108-109	❖ Zech. 3.2, Num. 9.23, Deut. 6.4 ⇄ Ps. 91.1

Catalogue 123

	QUOTATION	MT/TARGUM	BOWL	PUBLICATION	COMMENTS
C	Ps. 10.16 ⇄ Ps. 93.1 ⇄	Ps. 10.16	MS 1927/8	JBA 1	Liturgical response, *Pəsûgê dəzimrāʾ*: *Yəhî kavôd*
E	Exod. 15.18				**EC:** Exod. 15.3, Ps. 24.8, Ps. 10.16 ↔ Ps. 93.1 ↔ Exod. 15.18
P	יהוה מ[לך יהוה] מלך יהוה י[מלוך] לעד	יְהוָה מֶלֶךְ עוֹלָם וָעֶד אָבְדוּ גוֹיִם מֵאַרְצוֹ			Invoked as name of power: בעזמרה ד Other Quotations: Ps. 104.20
C	Ps. 10.16 ⇄ Ps. 93.1 ⇄	Ps. 10.16	MS 1927/45	JBA 3	See above
E	Exod. 15.18				
P	יהוה מ[לא יהוה] מלך יהוה ה[מלך] לע[ולם ו]עד	יְהוָה מֶלֶךְ עוֹלָם וָעֶד אָבְדוּ גוֹיִם מֵאַרְצוֹ			

	QUOTATION	MT/TARGUM	BOWL	PUBLICATION	COMMENTS
C	Ps. 10.16 ⇌ Ps. 93.1	Ps. 10.16	MS 1927/47	JBA 4	See above
E	Exod. 15.18				
P	יה[וה מלך יהוה] מלך יה[וה ימלך לעולם ועד]	יְהוָה מֶלֶךְ עוֹלָם וָעֶד׃ כָּל אָבְדוּ גוֹיִם מֵאַרְצוֹ׃			
C	Ps. 10.16 ⇌ Ps. 93.1	Ps. 10.16	MS 1927/64	JBA 5	See above
E	Exod. 15.18				Other Quotations:
P	מאבד י[ה]וה מלך יה[י] יהוה מלך לעולם ועד	יְהוָה מֶלֶךְ עוֹלָם וָעֶד׃ כָּל אָבְדוּ גוֹיִם מֵאַרְצוֹ׃			Ps. 104.20, Zech. 3.2
C	Ps. 10.16 ⇌ Ps. 93.1	Ps. 10.16	MS 2053/10	JBA 6	See above
E	Exod. 15.18				Cartouche
P	יהוה מלך יהוה מאבד	יְהוָה מֶלֶךְ עוֹלָם וָעֶד׃ כָּל אָבְדוּ גוֹיִם מֵאַרְצוֹ׃			
C	Ps 10.16 ⇌ Ps. 93.1	Ps. 10.16	MS 2053/12	JBA 7	See above
E	Exod. 15.18				Cartouche
P	יהוה מלך יהוה מאבד	יְהוָה מֶלֶךְ עוֹלָם וָעֶד׃ כָּל אָבְדוּ גוֹיִם מֵאַרְצוֹ׃			

Catalogue

	QUOTATION	MT/TARGUM	BOWL	PUBLICATION	COMMENTS
C	Ps. 10.16 ⇌ Ps. 93.1 ⇌	Ps. 10.16	MS 2053/83	JBA 9	See above
E	Exod. 15.18				
P	יהוה מלך יהוה מלך יהוה	יְהוָה מֶלֶךְ עוֹלָם וָעֶד			
	ימלך לעולם ועד	מֵאַרְצוֹ			
C	Ps. 10.16 ⇌ Ps. 93.1 ⇌	Ps. 10.16	MS 2053/185	JBA 10	See above
E	Exod. 15.18				
P	יהו[ה מלך] יהוה מ[לך יהוה	יְהוָה מֶלֶךְ עוֹלָם וָעֶד			
	ימלך לעולם ועד	מֵאַרְצוֹ			
C	Ps. 10.16 ⇌ Ps. 93.1 ⇌	Ps. 10.16	M 156	Corpus: 115–116	See above
E	Exod. 15.18				
P	יהוה מלך יהוה מלך יהוה	יְהוָה מֶלֶךְ עוֹלָם וָעֶד			
	ימלך לעולם ועד	מֵאַרְצוֹ			
C	Ps. 10.16 ⇌ Ps. 93.1 ⇌	Ps. 10.16	LO.831	Bhayro 2014	See above
E	Exod. 15.18				
P	יהוה מלך יהוה מלך יהוה	יְהוָה מֶלֶךְ עוֹלָם וָעֶד			
	ימלך לעולם ועד	מֵאַרְצוֹ			

	QUOTATION	MT/TARGUM	BOWL	PUBLICATION	COMMENTS
C	Ps. 10.16 ⇄ Ps. 93.1 ⇄	Ps. 10.16	MS 2053/79	JBA 11	Liturgical response, *Pasûqê dəzimrāʾ*: *Yəhî kəvôd*
E	Exod. 15.18				EC: Exod. 15.3, Ps. 24.8, Ps. 10.16 ↔ Ps. 93.1 ↔ Exod. 15.18
P	יהו[י] מלך יהוה מל[ך] יהוה ימלוך לעלם ועד	מיהוה מלך יהוה מלך יהוה ימלך לעלם ועד			Invoked as name of power: במטבעה ד
C	Ps. 10.16 ⇄ Ps. 93.1 ⇄	Ps. 10.16	MS 2053/178	JBA 12	See above
E	Exod. 15.18				
P	יהוה מלך יהוה מלך יהוה ימלוך לעל[ו]ם [ועד]	מיהוה מלך יהוה מלך יהוה ימלך לעלם ועד			

	QUOTATION	MT/TARGUM	BOWL	PUBLICATION	COMMENTS
א	Ps. 24.8	Ps. 24.8	LO.831	Bhayro 2014	**EC:** Exod. 15.3, Ps. 24.8, Ps. 10.16 ↔ Ps. 93.1 ↔ Exod. 15.18
E	יהוה עזוז וגבור יהוה	מָן דֵּין מַלְכָּא יְקָרָא יְיָ			Invoked as name of power: בשמיה ד
P	מלחמה	תַּקִּיפָא וְגִבָּרָא יְיָ גִבָּרָא גָחֵין קְרָבָא			Other Quotations: Ps. 104.20
א	Ps. 24.8	Ps. 24.8	M 156	Corpus: 115-116	See above
E	יהוה עזוז וגבוד יהוה	מָן דֵּין מַלְכָּא יְקָרָא יְיָ			
P	מלחמה	תַּקִּיפָא וְגִבָּרָא יְיָ גִבָּרָא גָחֵין קְרָבָא			
א	Ps. 24.8	Ps. 24.8	MS 1927/8	JBA 1	See above
E	יהוה ג[בור עזוז] יהוה	מָן דֵּין מַלְכָּא יְקָרָא יְיָ			
P	[מלחמה]	תַּקִּיפָא וְגִבָּרָא יְיָ גִבָּרָא גָחֵין קְרָבָא			
א	Ps. 24.8	Ps. 24.8	MS 1927/45	JBA 3	See above
E	יהוה עזוז וגבו[ר] יהוה	מָן דֵּין מַלְכָּא יְקָרָא יְיָ			
P	ג[י]בר מלח[מה]	תַּקִּיפָא וְגִבָּרָא יְיָ גִבָּרָא גָחֵין קְרָבָא			

	QUOTATION	MT/TARGUM	BOWL	PUBLICATION	COMMENTS
M	Ps. 24.8	Ps. 24.8	MS 1927/47	JBA 4	See above
E	יהוה עזוז וגבור יהוה גב[ור]	מִי זֶה מֶלֶךְ הַכָּבוֹד יְהוָה עִזּוּז וְגִבּוֹר יְהוָה גִּבּוֹר מִלְחָמָה			
P	]מלח[מה				
M	Ps. 24.8	Ps. 24.8	MS 1927/64	JBA 5	See above
E	יהוה עז[וז] ו[גב]יבור יהוה	מִי זֶה מֶלֶךְ הַכָּבוֹד יְהוָה עִזּוּז וְגִבּוֹר יְהוָה גִּבּוֹר מִלְחָמָה			Other Quotations: Ps. 104.20, Zech. 3.2
P	ג[בו]ר מלחמה				
M	Ps. 24.8	Ps. 24.8	MS 2053/10	JBA 6	See above
E	יהוה עזוז וגבור יהוה	מִי זֶה מֶלֶךְ הַכָּבוֹד יְהוָה עִזּוּז וְגִבּוֹר יְהוָה גִּבּוֹר מִלְחָמָה			Cartouche
P	מלחמה				
M	Ps. 24.8	Ps. 24.8	MS 2053/12	JBA 7	See above
E	יהוה עזוז וגבור יהוה	מִי זֶה מֶלֶךְ הַכָּבוֹד יְהוָה עִזּוּז וְגִבּוֹר יְהוָה גִּבּוֹר מִלְחָמָה			Cartouche
P	מלחמה				
M	Ps. 24.8	Ps. 24.8	MS 2053/183	JBA 9	See above
E	יהוה עזוז וגבור יהוה	מִי זֶה מֶלֶךְ הַכָּבוֹד יְהוָה עִזּוּז וְגִבּוֹר יְהוָה גִּבּוֹר מִלְחָמָה			
P	מלחמה				

	QUOTATION	MT/TARGUM	BOWL	PUBLICATION	COMMENTS
א	Ps. 24.8	Ps. 24.8	MS 2053/185	JBA 10	See above
E	יהוה צבאות עזוז וגבור יהוה גבור מלחמה	מַן דֵין הוּא מַלְכָּא יְקָרָא יְיָ עַשִׁין וְגִיבָּר יְיָ גִיבָּר מַגִיחַ קְרָבִין			
P					
א	Ps. 24.8	Ps. 24.8	MS 2053/79	JBA 11	**EC:** Ps. 24.8, Exod. 15.3, Ps. 10.16 ↔ Ps. 93.1 ↔ Exod. 15.18
E	יהו[ה ג]בור יהוה[עז]וז וג[בור יהו]ה גבור מלחמה	מַן דֵין הוּא מַלְכָּא יְקָרָא יְיָ עַשִׁין וְגִיבָּר יְיָ גִיבָּר מַגִיחַ קְרָבִין			Invoked as name of power: בתשמיה ד
P					
א	Ps. 24.8	Ps. 24.8	MS 2053/178	JBA 12	See above
E	יהוה גבו[ר] עז[וז] וגבור יהוה גבור מלחמה	מַן דֵין הוּא מַלְכָּא יְקָרָא יְיָ עַשִׁין וְגִיבָּר יְיָ גִיבָּר מַגִיחַ קְרָבִין			
P					
א	Ps. 32.7	Ps. 32.7	MS 1928/1	JBA 55	✣ Ps. 32.7, Ps. 55.9
	אתה סתר לי מצר תצרני רני פלט תסובבני סלה	אַתְּ מְסַתְרָא לִי מִמְעִיק תִּנְטְרִנַנִי שִׁבְחִין דְפוּרְקָנָא תַחְזַרְנֵנִי לְעַלְמִין			

	QUOTATION	MT/TARGUM	BOWL	PUBLICATION	COMMENTS
א	Ps. 46.8 יהוה צבאות עמנו מ[שגב]לנו א[להי יעקב	Ps. 46.8 יְהוָה צְבָאוֹת עִמָּנוּ מִשְׂגָּב־לָנוּ אֱלֹהֵי יַעֲקֹב	BM 91763	Curses: 121-122 = CAMIB 41	For protection against a named individual ❖ Ps. 46.8, Ps. 86.5, Ps. 116.6
א p	Ps. 46.8 יעקב סלה [...]	Ps. 46.8 יְהוָה צְבָאוֹת עִמָּנוּ מִשְׂגָּב־לָנוּ אֱלֹהֵי יַעֲקֹב סֶלָה	VA 2509	Curses: 31-32	For protection against a named individual A large portion of the bowl is missing, but the parallel with BM 91763 allows the identification of ❖ Ps. 46.8, Ps. 86.5
א	Ps. 55.8 הנה [ה]רחק [נ]דד אלין אלינה במדבר סלה	Ps. 55.8 הִנֵּה הִרְחִיק נְדֹד אָלִין בַּמִּדְבָּר סֶלָה	MS 2053/196	JBA 103	❖ Ps. 55.8, Ps. 91.7 Other quotations: ❖ Num. 9.23, Zech. 3.2

	QUOTATION	MT/TARGUM	BOWL	PUBLICATION	COMMENTS
א	Ps. 55.9 אחישה מפלט לי מרוח סעה מסער	Ps. 55.9 אָחִישָׁה מִפְלָט לִי מֵרוּחַ סֹעָה מִסָּעַר׃	MS 1928/1	JBA 55	❖ Ps. 32.7, Ps. 55.9 Beneficiary's name inserted directly into the quotation
א	Ps. 55.9 אחיש[...] בן {בת} מפלט לה מרוח סעה	Ps. 55.9 אָחִישָׁה מִפְלָט לִי מֵרוּחַ סֹעָה מִסָּעַר׃	MS 2053/230	JBA 109	❖ Zech. 3.2, Ps. 55.9 Third person pronoun of the beneficiary inserted directly into the quotation
א P	Ps. 68.5 שירו לאלהים זמרו שמו	Ps. 68.5 שִׁירוּ לֵאלֹהִים זַמְּרוּ שְׁמוֹ סֹלּוּ לָרֹכֵב בָּעֲרָבוֹת בְּיָהּ שְׁמוֹ וְעִלְזוּ לְפָנָיו׃	MS 2053/236	Bohak 2012: 48-49	

QUOTATION	MT/TARGUM	BOWL	PUBLICATION	COMMENTS
Ps. 69.24	Ps. 69.24 תֶּחְשַׁכְנָה עֵינֵיהֶם מֵרְאוֹת וּמָתְנֵיהֶם תָּמִיד הַמְעַד	—	AMB 9	For cursing a named individual Other quotations: ✢ Ps. 69.24, Ps. 69.26, Exod. 22.23, Deut. 28.22, Deut. 28.35, Deut. 28.28, Lev. 26.29; ✢ Mic. 7.16-17, Deut. 29.19; [≅ Jer. 8.4 = Amos 8.14 ↔ Lev. 26.37]
הה קריום לאהלום אל ידי רשיה				
Ps. 69.26	Ps. 69.26 תְּהִי־טִירָתָם נְשַׁמָּה בְּאָהֳלֵיהֶם אַל־יְהִי יֹשֵׁב	—	AMB 9	See above
הה קריום נמשה אל ידי רשיה				

QUOTATION	MT/TARGUM	BOWL	PUBLICATION	COMMENTS
Ps. 72.18-19 ברוך יהוה אלהים אלהי ישראל עשה נפלאות לבדו וברוך שם כבודו לעולם וימלא כבודו את כל הארץ אמן ואמן	Ps. 72.18-19 בריך יהוה אלהא אלהא דישראל עבד פרישן בלחודוהי ובריך שום איקר מלכותיה לעלם ויתמלי מן איקר מלכותיה ית כל ארעא אמן ואמן	M 108	Corpus: 71	❖ Ps. 106.47 ⇌ 1 Chron. 16.35, Zech. 3.2, Ps. 89.53, Ps. 106.48, Ps. 72.18-19, Ps. 104.31 Cf. *Seder ʿAmram*: ʿArvit Invoked as name of power: בשום The bowl text consists almost solely of biblical verses
Ps. 86.5 כי אתה אדני טוב וסלח ורב חסד לכל קראיך	Ps. 86.5 ארום את יהוה טב שביק ושרי וסגי טיבו לכל דקריין לך	BM 91763	CAMIB 41 = Curses: 121-122	For protection against a named individual ❖ Ps. 46.8, Ps. 86.5, Ps. 116.6

	QUOTATION	MT/TARGUM	BOWL	PUBLICATION	COMMENTS
P	Ps. 86.5 כי אתה ה י(ה)וה[ן...]	Ps. 86.5 כִּי־אַתָּה אֲדֹנָי טוֹב וְסַלָּח וְרַב־חֶסֶד לְכָל־קֹרְאֶיךָ	VA 2509	Curses: 31-32	For protection against a named individual A large portion of the bowl is missing, but the parallel with BM 91763 allows the identification of ✢ Ps. 46.8, Ps. 86.5
א	Ps. 86.17 עשה עמי אות לטובה ויראו שנאי ויבשו כי אתה יהוה עזרתני ונחמתני	Ps. 86.17 עֲשֵׂה־עִמִּי אוֹת לְטוֹבָה וְיִרְאוּ שֹׂנְאַי וְיֵבֹשׁוּ כִּי־אַתָּה יְהוָה עֲזַרְתַּנִי וְנִחַמְתָּנִי	Moriah 2	Gordon 1984: 238	✢ 1 Sam. 2.2, Ps. 86.17 Tetragrammaton enclosed in a cartouche

QUOTATION	MT/TARGUM	BOWL	PUBLICATION	COMMENTS
Ps. 89.53 ברוך יהוה לעולם אמן ואמן	Ps. 89.53 בְּרוּךְ יְהֹוָה לְעוֹלָם אָמֵן וְאָמֵן	M 108	Corpus: 71	✣ Ps. 106.47 ⇄ 1 Chron. 16.35, Zech. 3.2, Ps. 89.53, Ps. 106.48, Ps. 72.18-19, Ps. 104.31 Cf. *Seder ʿAmram: ʿArvit* Invoked as name of power: בשום The bowl text consists almost solely of biblical verses
Ps. 91.1 ישב בסתר עליון בצל שדי יתלונן	Ps. 91.1 יֹשֵׁב בְּסֵתֶר עֶלְיוֹן בְּצֵל שַׁדַּי יִתְלוֹנָן	VA 2423	Curses: 37-39	For annuling the curses of several named individuals
Ps. 91.1 ישב בסתר עליון בצל שדי יתלונן יתלונן שדי בצל עליון בסתר ישב	Ps. 91.1 יֹשֵׁב בְּסֵתֶר עֶלְיוֹן בְּצֵל שַׁדַּי יִתְלוֹנָן	JNF 124	Ford 2016: 153-154	✣ Deut. 6.4, Ps. 91.1, Exod. 14.31 Repeated in reverse order

QUOTATION	MT/TARGUM	BOWL	PUBLICATION	COMMENTS
Ps. 91.1 ⇄ Deut. 6.4 שמע ישראל יהוה אלהינו יהוה אחד שמע ישראל יהוה בצל שדי יתלונן אחד יהוה	Ps. 91.1 יֹשֵׁב בְּסֵתֶר עֶלְיוֹן בְּצֵל שַׁדַּי יִתְלוֹנָן	JHMB 242/1	AMB 11	✜ Zech. 3.2, Deut. 6.4 ⇄ Ps. 91.1
Ps. 91.1 ⇄ Deut. 6.4 [יהוה בסתר] שמע ישראל יהוה עליון בצל שדי יתלונן אלהינו יהוה אחד	Ps. 91.1 יֹשֵׁב בְּסֵתֶר עֶלְיוֹן בְּצֵל שַׁדַּי יִתְלוֹנָן	Louvre AOD 361	Schwab 1891: 592	Other quotations: Zech. 3.2 Partial edition of the bowl text
Ps. 91.1 ⇄ Deut. 6.4 יהוה בסתר שמע ישראל יהוה עליון בצל שדי יתלונן אלהינו יהוה אח(ד)	Ps. 91.1 יֹשֵׁב בְּסֵתֶר עֶלְיוֹן בְּצֵל שַׁדַּי יִתְלוֹנָן	Aaron B	Geller 1986: 108-109	✜ Zech. 3.2, Num. 9.23, Deut. 6.4 ⇄ Ps. 91.1
Ps. 91.1 ⇄ Deut. 6.4 שמע ישראל יהוה בסתר	Ps. 91.1 יֹשֵׁב בְּסֵתֶר עֶלְיוֹן בְּצֵל שַׁדַּי יִתְלוֹנָן	ZRL 48	Gordon 1978: 233	Other quotations: Zech. 3.2

QUOTATION	MT/TARGUM	BOWL	PUBLICATION	COMMENTS
Ps. 91.7	Ps. 91.7	İstanbul Arkeoloji Müzeleri 5365	Isbell 52 = Gordon C	❖ Ps. 91.7, Ps. 91.10 CF: כתיב
	יפול מצדך [אלף] ורבבה לפה ימינך אליך לא יגש			
Ps. 91.7	Ps. 91.7	MS 2053/196	JBA 103	❖ Ps. 55.8, Ps. 91.7 Other quotations: ❖ Num. 9.23, Zech. 3.2
	יפול מצדך אלף ורבבה לפה ימינך אליך לא יגש			
Ps. 91.10	Ps. 91.10	İstanbul Arkeoloji Müzeleri 5365	Isbell 52 = Gordon C	❖ Ps. 91.7, Ps. 91.10 CF: כתיב
	לא תאנה אליך רעה ונגע לא יקרב באהלך			

QUOTATION	MT/TARGUM	BOWL	PUBLICATION	COMMENTS
Ps. 91.11 בְּכָל דְּרָכֶיךָ מְטַלָּלֶי לָךְ אֲנָא אָמַר לָךְ לִמְחַלְפָנָא	Ps. 91.11 בְּכָל דְּרָכֶיךָ מְטַלָּלֶי לָךְ יַצִי	S-442	SHM 1	CF: בה אנבלהנא אמרה ל[ך], אמרנא 'To you, Maḥlefana s. Rewiṯa, I say.'
Ps. 91.11 בְּכָל דְּרָכֶיךָ מְטַלָּלֶי לָךְ יַצִי (א)מָר	Ps. 91.11 בְּכָל דְּרָכֶיךָ מְטַלָּלֶי לָךְ יַצִי	M 6	Shaked 1995: 211-213	✣ Num. 9.23, Zech. 3.2, Ezek. 32.27, Ps. 91.11
Ps. 91.11 בְּכָל דְּרָכֶיךָ מְטַלָּלֶי לָךְ הוצַי יַצִי[מ]רוך	Ps. 91.11 בְּכָל דְּרָכֶיךָ מְטַלָּלֶי לָךְ יַצִי	M 164	Levene 2007	✣ Isa. 50.11, Ps. 116.6, Ps. 91.11 Other quotations: Dan. 7.11, Exod. 23.21 The bowl text also quotes m. Šebu. 4.13

C   Ps. 93.1 ⇌ Ps. 10.16 ⇌   SEE Ps. 10.16 ABOVE
E   Exod. 15.18   [12 ENTRIES]
P

Catalogue

QUOTATION	MT/TARGUM	BOWL	PUBLICATION	COMMENTS
Ps. 104.20 תשת חשך ויהי [ל]ילה בו תרמש כל חיתו יער	Ps. 104.20 תָּשֶׁת חֹשֶׁךְ וִיהִי לָיְלָה בּוֹ תִרְמֹשׂ כָּל חַיְתוֹ יָעַר	MS 1927/8	JBA 1	**CF:** קרבאה דהכיב Other Quotations: [EC:] Exod. 15.3, Ps. 24.8, Ps. 10.16 ↔ Ps. 93.1 ↔ Exod. 15.18
Ps. 104.20 תשת חשך ויהי לילה בו תרמש כל חיתו יאר	Ps. 104.20 תָּשֶׁת חֹשֶׁךְ וִיהִי לָיְלָה בּוֹ תִרְמֹשׂ כָּל חַיְתוֹ יָעַר	MS 1927/29	JBA 2	See above
Ps. 104.20 תשת חשך ויהי [ל]ילה[ז] בו תרמש כל חיתו יער	Ps. 104.20 תָּשֶׁת חֹשֶׁךְ וִיהִי לָיְלָה בּוֹ תִרְמֹשׂ כָּל חַיְתוֹ יָעַר	MS 1927/45	JBA 3	See above
Ps. 104.20 תשת חשך ויהי לילה בו תרמש כל חיתו יער	Ps. 104.20 תָּשֶׁת חֹשֶׁךְ וִיהִי לָיְלָה בּוֹ תִרְמֹשׂ כָּל חַיְתוֹ יָעַר	MS 1927/47	JBA 4	See above
Ps. 104.20 תשת חשך ויהי לילה בו תרמש כל חיתו יער	Ps. 104.20 תָּשֶׁת חֹשֶׁךְ וִיהִי לָיְלָה בּוֹ תִרְמֹשׂ כָּל חַיְתוֹ יָעַר	MS 1927/64	JBA 5	See above Other Quotations: Zech. 3.2

QUOTATION	MT/TARGUM	BOWL	PUBLICATION	COMMENTS
Ps. 104.20 תשת חש[ו]ך ויהי לילה בו תרמש כל חיתו יאר	Ps. 104.20 תָּֽשֶׁת־חֹשֶׁךְ וִיהִי לָיְלָה בּֽוֹ־תִרְמֹשׂ כׇּל־חַיְתוֹ־יָֽעַר	MS 2053/10	JBA 6	See above
Ps. 104.20 תשת חושך ויהי לילה בו תרמש כל חיתו יאר	Ps. 104.20 תָּֽשֶׁת־חֹשֶׁךְ וִיהִי לָיְלָה בּֽוֹ־תִרְמֹשׂ כׇּל־חַיְתוֹ־יָֽעַר	MS 2053/12	JBA 7	See above
Ps. 104.20 תשת חושך ויהי לילה בו תרמש כל חיתו יאר	Ps. 104.20 תָּֽשֶׁת־חֹשֶׁךְ וִיהִי לָיְלָה בּֽוֹ־תִרְמֹשׂ כׇּל־חַיְתוֹ־יָֽעַר	MS 2053/83	JBA 9	See above
Ps. 104.20 ת[ש]ת חוש[ך] ויהי לילה ב[ו] תר[מש כל] חיתו יער	Ps. 104.20 תָּֽשֶׁת־חֹשֶׁךְ וִיהִי לָיְלָה בּֽוֹ־תִרְמֹשׂ כׇּל־חַיְתוֹ־יָֽעַר	MS 2053/185	JBA 10	See above
Ps. 104.20 תשת חושך ויהי לילה בו תרמש כל חיתו יאר	Ps. 104.20 תָּֽשֶׁת־חֹשֶׁךְ וִיהִי לָיְלָה בּֽוֹ־תִרְמֹשׂ כׇּל־חַיְתוֹ־יָֽעַר	M 156	Corpus: 115-116	See above

QUOTATION	MT/TARGUM	BOWL	PUBLICATION	COMMENTS
Ps. 104.20	Ps. 104.20 תְּשֶׁת חֹשֶׁךְ וִיהִי לַיְלָה בּוֹ תִרְמֹשׂ כָּל חַיְתוֹ יָעַר [תהי חשך ויהי] ליליא ביה רחשין כל חיות [חורשא]	LO.831	Bhayro 2014	See above
Ps. 104.20	Ps. 104.20 תְּשֶׁת חֹשֶׁךְ וִיהִי לַיְלָה בּוֹ תִרְמֹשׂ כָּל חַיְתוֹ יָעַר תהי חשך ויהי ליליא ביה [כל חיות יער]	MS 2053/55	JBA 8	The writing is extremely faded
Ps. 104.31	Ps. 104.31 יְהִי כְבוֹד יְהוָה לְעוֹלָם יִשְׂמַח יְהוָה בְּמַעֲשָׂיו יהי יקרא דיהוה לעלם יחדי יהוה בעובדוי	M 108	Corpus: 71	✢ Ps. 106.47 ⇄ 1 Chron. 16.35, Zech. 3.2, Ps. 89.53, Ps. 106.48, Ps. 72.18-19, Ps. 104.31 Cf. Seder ʿAmram: ʿArvit Invoked as name of power: בשום The bowl text consists almost solely of biblical verses

QUOTATION	MT/TARGUM	BOWL	PUBLICATION	COMMENTS
א Ps. 106.47 ⇄ 1 Chron. ג 16.35 והושיענו והצילנו יהוה ותקבצנו מן מלכותה דעמה עד להודות לשם קדש(י)ך להשתבח(ב)תה	Ps. 106.47 הוֹשִׁיעֵנוּ ׀ יְהוָה אֱלֹהֵינוּ וְקַבְּצֵנוּ מִן־הַגּוֹיִם לְהֹדוֹת לְשֵׁם קָדְשֶׁךָ לְהִשְׁתַּבֵּחַ בִּתְהִלָּתֶךָ	M 108	Corpus: 71	See above
א Ps. 106.48 ברוך יהוה אלהי ישראל מן עלמא ועד עלמא יאמר כל עמא אמן הללויה	Ps. 106.48 בָּרוּךְ־יְהוָה אֱלֹהֵי יִשְׂרָאֵל מִן־הָעוֹלָם ׀ וְעַד הָעוֹלָם וְאָמַר כָּל־הָעָם אָמֵן הַלְלוּ־יָהּ	M 108	Corpus: 71	✥ Ps. 106.47 ⇄ 1 Chron. 16.35, Zech. 3.2, Ps. 89.53, Ps. 106.48, Ps. 72.18-19, Ps. 104.31 Cf. *Seder 'Amram: 'Arvit* Invoked as name of power: בשם The bowl text consists almost solely of biblical verses

QUOTATION	MT/TARGUM	BOWL	PUBLICATION	COMMENTS
Ps. 114.3 [...] אמ׳ יתיה חמ[י]ה הוא ים	Ps. 114.3 (Tg. Ket.) ימא חזא ואזל ירדנא אסתחר לאחורוי	MS 1927/50	JBA 116	Unknown targum Other quotations: Exod. 14.31, Isa. 6.3
Ps. 115.1-2 {הוה} לנא לא יהוה לנא לא למנה למה יאמרו בה יהוה לשמך תן יקרא על חסידך על קושטך למה יימרון עממיא אן אלהכון הוא	Ps. 115.1-2 לָא לָנוּ יְיָ לֹא לָנוּ כִּי לְשִׁמְךָ תֵּן כָּבוֹד עַל חַסְדְּךָ עַל אֲמִתֶּךָ. לָמָּה יֹאמְרוּ הַגּוֹיִם אַיֵּה נָא אֱלֹהֵיהֶם׃ (MT) לא לתושבחתן יי אלא לשמך הב יקרא על טיבותך על קושטך למא יימרון עממיא אן אלהא דנהון (Tg. Ket.)	—	Shaked 2015: 109-110	Unknown targum Other quotations: Isa. 51.15 = Jer. 31.34

	QUOTATION	MT/TARGUM	BOWL	PUBLICATION	COMMENTS
א	Ps. 116.6 שֹׁמֵר פְּתָאיִם יְהוָה דַּלּוֹתִי	Ps. 116.6 שֹׁמֵר פְּתָאיִם יְהוָה דַּלּוֹתִי וְלִי יְהוֹשִׁיעַ׃	BM 91763	CAMIB 41 = Curses: 121-122	For protection against a named individual ❖ Ps. 46.8, Ps. 86.5, Ps. 116.6
א ב	Ps. 116.6 שמור פתם [י]ה[ות]	Ps. 116.6 שֹׁמֵר פְּתָאיִם יְהוָה דַּלּוֹתִי וְלִי יְהוֹשִׁיעַ׃	MS 1928/8	JBA 56	
א ב	Ps. 116.6 שמר פתאים יהוה דלותי פתאם	Ps. 116.6 שֹׁמֵר פְּתָאיִם יְהוָה דַּלּוֹתִי וְלִי יְהוֹשִׁיעַ׃	M 164	Levene 2007	❖ Isa. 50.11, Ps. 116.6, Ps. 91.11 Repeated in reverse order Other quotations: Dan. 7.11, Exod. 23.21 The bowl text also quotes m. Šebu. 4.13

QUOTATION	MT/TARGUM	BOWL	PUBLICATION	COMMENTS
Ps. 121.4	Ps. 121.4 הִנֵּה לֹא יָנוּם וְלֹא יִישָׁן שׁוֹמֵר יִשְׂרָאֵל	IM 76752	Faraj 2021	Other quotations: Num. 6.24-26; Ps 121.7
Ps. 121.7	Ps. 121.7 יְהוָה יִשְׁמָרְךָ מִכָּל רָע יִשְׁמֹר אֶת נַפְשֶׁךָ	CBS 9009	AIT 12	The final line of the bowl text, which quotes Ps. 121.7, appears to have faded considerably since Montgomery (1913) produced his transcription and hand copy (pl. xiii) of the bowl. Montgomery's reading is preserved in square brackets.

QUOTATION	MT/TARGUM	BOWL	PUBLICATION	COMMENTS
P Ps. 121.7 יהוה ישמרך מכל רע ישמר הבהמה והחיה...	Ps. 121.7 יְהוָה יִשְׁמָרְךָ מִכָּל־רָע יִשְׁמֹר אֶת־נַפְשֶׁךָ	IM 76752	Faraj 2021	Final words of the verse (ישמר את נפשך) emended to include a list of the beneficiary's property Other quotations: Num. 6.24-26; Ps 121.4
⚘ Ps. 121.7-8 יהוה ישמרך מכל רע {נ} יהוה ישמר ית נפשך יהוה ישמר צאתך ובואך מן [כדו ואנה] עד ע[ל]ם	Ps. 121.7-8 יְהוָה יִשְׁמָרְךָ מִכָּל־רָע יִשְׁמֹר אֶת־נַפְשֶׁךָ׃ יְהוָה יִשְׁמָר־צֵאתְךָ וּבוֹאֶךָ מֵעַתָּה וְעַד־עוֹלָם׃	MS 2053/56	JBA 67	❖ Ps. 121.7-8, Zech. 3.2 Other quotations: ❖ Exod. 3.15, Isa. 40.31; ❖ Isa. 60.11 ↔ Gen. 27.28 (T)

QUOTATION	MT/TARGUM	BOWL	PUBLICATION	COMMENTS
Ps. 121.7-8	Ps. 121.7-8 יהוה ישמר [ת]משי עה מכל רע ישמר את נפשך יהוה ישמר צאתך ובואך [...] ידידי מעתה ועד עולם	C10-116	Franco 1978/1979: 236-237	The writing is extremely faded. The name of the beneficiary (Didoy) appears to have been inserted directly into the quotation
Ps. 125.2	Ps. 125.2 {ירושלם} הרים סביב לה ויהוה סביב לעמו מעתה ועד עולם	IM 5497	Isbell 19 = Gordon G	
Ps. 125.2	Ps. 125.2 יהוה סביב לעמו מעתה ועד עולם	MS 1927/14	JBA 113	✣ Isa. 50.11, Ps. 125.2. Beneficiary's name and property inserted directly into the quotation

148   *The Bible in the Bowls*

	QUOTATION	MT/TARGUM	BOWL	PUBLICATION	COMMENTS
א	Prov. 3.4 ומצא חן ושכל טוב בעיני אלהים ואדם	Prov. 3.4 וּמְצָא־חֵ֥ן וְשֵֽׂכֶל־ט֑וֹב בְּעֵינֵ֥י אֱלֹהִ֖ים וְאָדָֽם׃	MS 1927/2	Shaked 2005: 25-26	For favour and success (in court) CF: נאבד
א S	Prov. 30.17	Prov. 30.17 עַ֤יִן ׀ תִּֽלְעַ֣ג לְאָב֮ וְתָב֪וּז לִֽיקֲּהַ֫ת־אֵ֥ם יִקְּר֥וּהָ עֹרְבֵי־נַ֑חַל וְֽיֹאכְל֥וּהָ בְנֵי־נָֽשֶׁר׃	IM 141803	Faraj 2010: 206-207	✢ Exod. 15.14-17 (Exod. 15.14 x2), Zech. 3.2, Prov. 30.17 The text of the bowl is divided into four sections arranged around a drawing of a demonic figure.
א P	Prov. 30.17	Prov. 30.17 עַ֤יִן ׀ תִּֽלְעַ֣ג לְאָב֮ וְתָב֪וּז לִֽיקֲּהַ֫ת־אֵ֥ם יִקְּר֥וּהָ עֹרְבֵי־נַ֑חַל וְֽיֹאכְל֥וּהָ בְנֵי־נָֽשֶׁר׃	M 4	Shaked 2006: 373-374	

QUOTATION	MT/TARGUM	BOWL	PUBLICATION	COMMENTS
Song 3.7 הנה מטתו שלשלמה ששים גברים סביב לה {ל} מגברי ישראל	Song 3.7 הִנֵּה מִטָּתוֹ שֶׁלִּשְׁלֹמֹה שִׁשִּׁים גִּבֹּרִים סָבִיב לָהּ מִגִּבֹּרֵי יִשְׂרָאֵל	BM 91765	Isbell 66 = CAMIB 26	❖ Song 3.7, Num. 6.24-26, Isa. 44.25
Song 3.7-8 הנה [מטת ש]לומה ששים גברים סביבה [ל]ה אשר מגברי ישראל [אחוז] חרב מלמדי מלחמה [א'] גבר חרבו	Song 3.7-8 הִנֵּה מִטָּתוֹ שֶׁלִּשְׁלֹמֹה שִׁשִּׁים גִּבֹּרִים סָבִיב לָהּ מִגִּבֹּרֵי יִשְׂרָאֵל. כֻּלָּם אֲחֻזֵי חֶרֶב מְלֻמְּדֵי מִלְחָמָה אִישׁ חַרְבּוֹ עַל יְרֵכוֹ מִפַּחַד בַּלֵּילוֹת	JNL Heb. 4 6079	AMB 12a = Ford 2016: 149	Other quotations: Isa. 40.12

QUOTATION	MT/TARGUM	BOWL	PUBLICATION	COMMENTS
Dan. 3.6	Dan. 3.6	S-447	SHM 5	'And may he (the chief of God's encampments) cast it (the evil spirit oppressing the beneficiary) "into the furnace of blazing fire" and to the flame of fire.'
≈ ומשדי ליה ית דר יקידתא ולשלהביתא דאשתא	P וּמַן־דִּי־לָא יִפֵּל יִסְגֻּד בַּהּ־שַׁעֲתָא יִתְרְמֵא לְגוֹא־אַתּוּן נוּרָא יָקִדְתָּא׃			
Dan. 3.6	Dan. 3.6	CBS 16017[59]	AIT 14	'And you (malevolent forces) "shall be cast into the burning fire" and to the flame of fire.'
≈ ותרמון לגוא אתון נורא יקידתא ולשלהביתא דאשתא	P וּמַן־דִּי־לָא יִפֵּל יִסְגֻּד בַּהּ־שַׁעֲתָא יִתְרְמֵא לְגוֹא־אַתּוּן נוּרָא יָקִדְתָּא׃			

---

[59] Montgomery (1913) mislabels the bowl as CBS 16917.

	QUOTATION	MT/TARGUM	BOWL	PUBLICATION	COMMENTS
ℵ	Dan. 7.11	Dan. 7.11	M 164	Levene 2007	Invoked as name of power: בשם
P					
E	בשם מטה חוה אחד אלהא קטילת חיותא והובד גשמה ויהיבת ליקדת אשא	חָזֵה הֲוֵית בֵּאדַיִן מִן־קָל מִלַּיָּא רַבְרְבָתָא דִּי קַרְנָא מְמַלֱלָה חָזֵה הֲוֵית עַד דִּי קְטִילַת חֵיוְתָא וְהוּבַד גִּשְׁמַהּ וִיהִיבַת לִיקֵדַת אֶשָּׁא׃			Other quotations: ✥ Isa. 50.11, Ps. 116.6, Ps. 91.11; Exod. 23.21 The bowl text also quotes m. Šebu. 4.13
ℵ	Neh. 9.32a = Deut. 10.17a	Neh. 9.32a	M 102	Curses: 108-109	For overturning and returning curses upon two/three named individuals
P					
E	האל הגדול הגבור והנורא	הָאֵל הַגָּדוֹל הַגִּבּוֹר וְהַנּוֹרָא שׁוֹמֵר הַבְּרִית וָחֶסֶד			EC Shemʿa, First Blessing Invoked as name of power: בשם ... והנורא

QUOTATION	MT/TARGUM	BOWL	PUBLICATION	COMMENTS
C 1 Chron. 16.35 ⇄ Ps. 106.47	1 Chron. 16.35 וְאִמְר֕וּ הוֹשִׁיעֵ֙נוּ֙ אֱלֹהֵ֣י יִשְׁעֵ֔נוּ וְקַבְּצֵ֥נוּ וְהַצִּילֵ֖נוּ מִן־הַגּוֹיִ֑ם לְהֹדוֹת֙ לְשֵׁ֣ם קָדְשֶׁ֔ךָ לְהִשְׁתַּבֵּ֖חַ בִּתְהִלָּתֶֽךָ	M 108	Corpus: 71	✣ Ps. 106.47 ⇄ 1 Chron. 16.35, Zech. 3.2, Ps. 89.53, Ps. 106.48, Ps. 72.18-19, Ps. 104.31 Cf. *Seder ʿAmram*: *ʿArvit* The bowl text consists almost solely of biblical verses
א 1 Chron. 29.10 P ברוך אתה יהוה אלהי ישראל	1 Chron. 29.10 וַיְבָ֣רֶךְ דָּוִ֣יד אֶת־יְהוָ֗ה לְעֵינֵ֖י כָּל־הַקָּהָ֑ל וַיֹּ֣אמֶר דָּוִ֗יד בָּר֨וּךְ אַתָּ֤ה יְהוָה֙ אֱלֹהֵי֙ יִשְׂרָאֵ֣ל אָבִ֔ינוּ מֵעוֹלָ֖ם וְעַד־עוֹלָֽם	IM 9745	Isbell 50 = Gordon E	
א 1 Chron. 29.10 P ברוך אתה יהוה אלהי ישראל	1 Chron. 29.10 וַיְבָ֣רֶךְ דָּוִ֣יד אֶת־יְהוָ֗ה לְעֵינֵ֖י כָּל־הַקָּהָ֑ל וַיֹּ֣אמֶר דָּוִ֗יד בָּר֨וּךְ אַתָּ֤ה יְהוָה֙ אֱלֹהֵי֙ יִשְׂרָאֵ֣ל אָבִ֔ינוּ מֵעוֹלָ֖ם וְעַד־עוֹלָֽם	IM 9746	Isbell 51 = Gordon F	

TABLE SHOWING THE DISTRIBUTION OF BIBLICAL QUOTATIONS IN PUBLISHED JBA INCANTATION BOWLS

The table below shows the distribution of biblical quotations across the corpus of published JBA bowl texts. For the sake of convenience, it is organised initially by major publications of large corpora (which overlap in a number of cases with large public and private collections of bowls).[1] Thereafter it is organised by the collections in which published bowls are held. Publication (author/year) and/or the sequence number or catalogue number of the bowl are given in the first column, followed by the quotation(s) included in each bowl text, and then the total number of quotations in the bowl text.

Table of Distribution of Biblical Quotations

Isbell 1975 (incl. Montgomery 1913 = AIT) [15/72]

Isbell 8 = AIT 3	Zech. 3.2	1
Isbell 9 = AIT 14	Dan. 3.6	1
Isbell 10 = AIT 5	Zech. 3.2	1
Isbell 12 = AIT 8	Exod. 3.15	1
Isbell 19 = Gordon G	Ps. 125.2	1

---

[1] Due to the vicissitudes of their publication history, note that two bowls appear twice in the table (HS 3005 = Isbell 55 = ZHS 5 = Ford and Morgenstern 2020: 19–20; and BM 91765 = Isbell 66 = CAMIB 26).

© 2022 James Waller, CC BY-NC 4.0   https://doi.org/10.11647/OBP.0305.03

Isbell 1975 (incl. Montgomery 1913 = AIT) [15/72]

Isbell 23 = AIT 12	Ps. 121.7	1
Isbell 24 = AIT 16	Zech. 3.2	1
Isbell 33	Isa. 6.3	1
Isbell 35 = AIT 26	Num. 9.23, Deut. 6.4, Hos. 2.2-4, Zech. 3.2	4
Isbell 42	Zech. 3.2	1
Isbell 50 = Gordon E	1 Chron. 29.10	1
Isbell 51 = Gordon F	1 Chron. 29.10	1
Isbell 52 = Gordon C	Ps. 91.7, Ps. 91.10	2
Isbell 55 = HS 3005	Num. 9.23	1
Isbell 66 = CAMIB 26	Num. 6.24-26, Isa. 44.25, Song 3.7	3

Naveh and Shaked 1985 and 1993 [7/22]

AMB 3	Num. 10.35	1
AMB 9	Exod. 22.23, Lev. 26.29, Deut. 28.22, Deut. 28.28, Deut. 28.35, Deut. 29.12, Mic. 7.16-17, Ps. 69.24, Ps. 69.26 [Lev. 26.37, Jer. 8.4 = Amos 8.14]	9[2]
AMB 11	Deut. 6.4, Ps. 91.1, Zech. 3.2	3
AMB 12a	Isa. 40.12, Song 3.7-8	2
AMB 12b	Isa. 40.12	1
AMB 13	Exod. 15.7	1
MSF 22	Num. 9.23, Exek. 32.27	2

Segal 2000 (British Museum Collection) [8/75]

CAMIB 23	Zech. 3.2	1
CAMIB 26 = Isbell 66	Num. 6.24-26, Isa. 44.25, Song 3.7	3
CAMIB 35	Num. 10.35, Isa. 44.25	2
CAMIB 40	Deut. 29.22, Deut. 29.27	2
CAMIB 41	Ps. 46.8, Ps. 86.5, Ps. 116.6	3
CAMIB 43	Deut. 29.27 = Jer. 21.5	1
CAMIB 65	Exod. 15.18	1
CAMIB 71+72+73	Gen. 49.22, Isa. 40.12	2

Levene 2003 (Moussaieff Collection) [8/20]

M 59	Zech. 3.2	1
M 102	Deut. 10.17 = Neh. 9.32a	1
M 108	Zech. 3.2, Ps. 72.18-19, Ps. 89.53, Ps. 104.31, Ps. 106.48, Ps. 106.47 ⇄ 1 Chron. 16.35	7
M 117	Isa. 6.3 ⇄ 1 Sam. 17.45, Isa. 37.16	3
M 123	Exod. 3.5 (Tg. Onq.)	1
M 138	Exod. 3.5 (Tg. Onq.)	1
M 142	Num. 14.9, Num. 32.33, Isa. 40.31	3
M 155	Isa. 45.2	1
M 156	Exod. 15.3, Ps. 24.8, Ps. 104.20, Ps. 10.16 ⇄ Ps. 93.1 ⇄ Exod. 15.18	3[1]

Levene 2013 (Vorderasiatisches Museum) [4/14]

VA 2416 = Curses: 46-47	2 Kgs 19.15	1
VA 2423 = Curses: 37-39	Ps. 91.1	1
VA 2484 = Curses: 22-24	Deut. 6.19	1
VA 2509 = Curses 31-32	Ps. 46.8, Ps. 86.5	2

Shaked, Ford, and Bhayro 2013 (Schøyen Collection, vol. 1) [19/64]

JBA 1	Exod. 15.3, Ps. 24.8, Ps. 104.20, Ps. 10.16 ⇄ Ps. 93.1 ⇄ Exod. 15.18	3[1]
JBA 2	Exod. 15.3, Ps. 104.20	2
JBA 3	Exod. 15.3, Ps. 24.8, Ps. 104.20, Ps. 10.16 ⇄ Ps. 93.1 ⇄ Exod. 15.18	3[1]
JBA 4	Exod. 15.3, Ps. 24.8, Ps. 104.20, Ps. 10.16 ⇄ Ps. 93.1 ⇄ Exod. 15.18	3[1]
JBA 5	Exod. 15.3, Ps. 24.8, Ps. 104.20, Ps. 10.16 ⇄ Ps. 93.1 ⇄ Exod. 15.18	3[1]
JBA 6	Exod. 15.3, Ps. 24.8, Ps. 104.20, Ps. 10.16 ⇄ Ps. 93.1 ⇄ Exod. 15.18	3[1]
JBA 7	Exod. 15.3, Ps. 24.8, Ps. 104.20, Ps. 10.16 ⇄ Ps. 93.1 ⇄ Exod. 15.18	3[1]
JBA 8	Ps. 104.20	1

Shaked, Ford, and Bhayro 2013 (Schøyen Collection, vol. 1) [19/64]

JBA 9	Exod. 15.3, Ps. 24.8, Ps. 104.20, Ps. 10.16 ⇄ Ps. 93.1 ⇄ Exod. 15.18	3[1]
JBA 10	Exod. 15.3, Ps. 24.8, Ps. 104.20, Ps. 10.16 ⇄ Ps. 93.1 ⇄ Exod. 15.18	3[1]
JBA 11	Exod. 15.3, Ps. 24.8, Ps. 10.16 ⇄ Ps. 93.1 ⇄ Exod. 15.18	2[1]
JBA 12	Exod. 15.3, Ps. 24.8 Ps. 10.16 ⇄ Ps. 93.1 ⇄ Exod. 15.18	2[1]
JBA 15	Exod. 3.15	1
JBA 31	Num. 9.23	1
JBA 42	Num. 9.23, Num. 10.36	2
JBA 46	Deut. 28.57	1
JBA 55	Ps. 32.7, Ps. 55.9	2
JBA 56	Ps. 116.6	1
JBA 60	Exod. 3.15	1

Shaked, Ford, and Bhayro 2022 (Schøyen Collection, vol. 2) [16/55]

JBA 65	Exod. 3.15, Isa. 40.31, Isa. 60.11, Gen. 27.28 (Tg. Onq.)	4
JBA 67	Exod. 3.15, Isa. 40.31, Isa. 60.11, Gen. 27.28 (Tg. Onq.), Ps. 121.7-8, Zech. 3.2	6

Shaked, Ford, and Bhayro 2022 (Schøyen Collection, vol. 2) [16/55]

JBA 73	Num. 9.23	1
JBA 75	Num. 9.23	1
JBA 87	Gen. 49.18	1
JBA 90	Isa. 12.3	1
JBA 95	Exod. 3.15, Isa. 40.31, Isa. 60.11, Gen. 27.28 (Tg. Onq.)	4
JBA 98	Exod. 3.15, Isa. 40.31, Isa. 60.11, Gen. 27.28 (Tg. Onq.)	4
JBA 101	Exod. 3.15, Isa. 40.31, Isa. 60.11, Gen. 27.28 (Tg. Onq.)	4
JBA 103	Num. 9.23, Zech. 3.2, Ps. 55.8, Ps. 91.7	4
JBA 104	Zech. 3.2	1
JBA 108	Zech. 3.2, Num. 12.13	2
JBA 109	Zech. 3.2, Ps. 55.9	2
JBA 113	Isa. 50.11, Ps. 125.2	2
JBA 114	Isa. 50.11	1
JBA 116	Exod. 14.31, Ps. 114.3, Isa. 6.3	3

Ford and Morgenstern 2020 = Müller-Kessler 2005 (Hilprecht Sammlung) [5/30]

HS 3003	Isa. 40.12	1
HS 3005	Num. 9.23	1
HS 3022	Num. 9.23, Num. 11.2, Num. 12.13	3

Ford and Morgenstern 2020 = Müller-Kessler 2005 (Hilprecht Sammlung) [5/30]

HS 3027	Deut. 6.4-9, Deut. 11.13-14	2
HS 3030	Exod. 19.9-12	1

Smaller Publications (Various Collections)

Aaron B = Geller 1986: 108	Num. 9.23, Deut. 6.4, Zech. 3.2, Ps. 91.1	4
Aaron E = Geller 1986:114	Isa. 40.13	1
Aaron F = Geller 1986: 115	Num. 9.23	1
IM 9736 = Saar 2013	Exod. 14.20	1
IM 56544 = ZHS 2a	Exod. 15.12	1
IM 76752 = Faraj 2021	Num. 6.24-26, Ps. 121.7, Ps. 121.4	3
IM 114987 = ZHS 4a	Isa. 40.12	1
IM 141803 = Faraj 2010	Exod. 15.14-17, Zech. 3.2, Prov. 30.17	3
IM 212092 = Al-Jubouri 2013	Isa. 37.16	1
IM 212093 = Al-Jubouri 2015	Isa. 37.16	1
IM 212103 = Al-Jubouri 2011	Isa. 37.16	1
M 1 = Shaked 1995: 207	Deut. 32.3, Isa. 6.3, Ezek. 1.5, Ezek. 1.27	4
M 4 = Shaked 2006: 373-374	Prov. 30.17	1
M 5 = Shaked 1999: 194	Gen. 49.22	1

Smaller Publications (Various Collections)

M 6 = Shaked 1995: 211-213	Num. 9.23, Ezek. 32.27, Zech. 3.2, Ps. 91.11	4
M 164 = Levene 2007	Exod. 23.21, Isa. 50.11, Ps. 91.11, Ps. 116.6, Dan. 7.11	5
MS 1927/2 = Shaked 2005: 25-26	Prov. 3.4	1
MS 1927/9 = Shaked 2005: 27	Exod. 3.15, Num. 6.24-26	2
MS 2053/7 = Bohak 2012: 47	Num. 10.35-36, Zech. 3.2	2
MS 2053/13 = Shaked 2011: 209	Num. 6.24-26, Zech. 3.2	2
MS 2053/159 = Corpus: 100-102	Exod. 15.16, Exod. 15.18, Isa. 6.3	3
MS 2053/216 = Corpus: 89-90	Exod. 3.5 (Tg. Onq.)	1
MS 2053/236 = Bohak 2012: 48-59	Ps. 68.5	1
MS 2053/257 = Shaked 2011: 210	Isa. 40.31	1
S-442 = SHM 1	Ps. 91.11	1
S-446 = SHM 4	Isa. 6.3	1
S-447 = SHM 5	Dan. 3.6	1
S-448 = SHM 6	Zech. 3.2	1

Smaller Publications (Various Collections)

T 15608 = Misgav 2018	Zech. 3.2	1
T 27987 = Misgav 2018	Deut. 6.4, Zech. 3.2	2
T 28001 = Misgav 2018	Zech. 3.2	1
VA 3854 = Levene 2003	Deut. 6.4-9, Deut. 11.13-21	2
VA 3853 = Levene 2003	[Deut. 6.4-6, Deut. 6.9], Deut. 11.13-21	2
A33965 = Kaufman 1973	Jer. 2.1, Jer. 2.2, Jer. 2.3, Ezek. 21.21-22	4
C10-116 = Franco 1978/1979: 236-237	Ps. 121.7-8	1
De Menil = Isbell 1976	Deut. 6.4	1
JNF 124 = Ford 2016: 153-154	Exod. 14.31, Deut. 6.4, Ps. 91.1	3
MFL 10895 = Bhayro 2017	Gen. 30.22, Zech. 3.2	2
Moriah 2 = Gordon 1984: 238	1 Sam. 2.2, Ps. 86.17	2
SD 34 = Levene/Bhayro 2005/6	Isa. 60.6, Isa. 60.8, Isa. 60.11	3
XI-t 5178 = Müller-Kessler 1994: B1	Isa. 40.12	1
Müller-Kessler 1994: B2	Isa. 40.12	1
ZRL 48 = Gordon 1978	Deut. 6.4, Zech. 3.2, Ps. 91.1	3

Smaller Publications (Various Collections)

Abousamra 2020	Zech. 3.2, Isa. 26.4	2
Ford/Ten-Ami 2012	Jer. 5.22	1
Herman 2021	Isa. 40.6-8	1
Müller-Kessler 2013	Deut. 6.4	1
Schwab 1891: 592	Deut. 6.4, Zech. 3.2, Ps. 91.1	3
Shaked 2015: 109-110	Isa. 51.15 = Jer. 31.34, Ps. 115.1-2	2

BIBLIOGRAPHY

Abousamra, Gaby. 2010. 'Une nouvelle coupe magique araméenne'. In *Magie et divination dans les cultures de l'Orient*, edited by J.-M. Durand and A. Jacqet, 109–121. Paris: Editions Jean Maisonneuve.

———. 2019. 'An Incantation Bowl from the Matenadaran'. *Semitica* 61: 139–146.

———. 2020. 'Semomit in a New Incantation Bowl'. In *Between the Worlds: Magic, Miracles, and Mysticism*, vol. 2, edited by M. Maeva, Y. Erolova, P. Stoyanova, M. Hristova, V. Ivanova, 455–464. Sofia: EFSEM – BAS and Paradigma.

Abousamra, Gaby, and André Lemaire. 2016. 'Bol magique avec inscription araméenne'. *Semitica* 58: 247–255.

Abudraham, Ohad. 2020. 'Features of the Hebrew Language on Babylonian Jewish Incantation Bowls'. *Leshonenu* 83: 24–58. (Hebrew)

Al-Jubouri, Bahaa Amer. 'An Aramaic Incantation Bowl in Iraq Museum'. *Sumer* 65: 25–30.

———. 2013. 'An Aramaic Incantation Text'. *Journal of Semitic Studies* 58: 59–63.

———. 2015. 'A New Aramaic Incantation Bowl'. *Semitica* 57: 211–216.

Andersen, Francis I. and A. Dean Forbes. 2013. 'Matres Lectionis: Biblical Hebrew.' In *Encyclopedia of Hebrew Language and Linguistics*, edited by Geoffrey Khan. Leiden: Brill. http://dx.doi.org/10.1163/2212-4241_ehll_EHLL_COM_00000286, accessed 26 November 2021.

Angel, Joseph. 2009. 'The Use of the Hebrew Bible in Early Jewish Magic'. *Religion Compass* 3 (5): 785–798.

Bar-Asher Siegal, Elitzur. 2013. *Introduction to the Grammar of Jewish Babylonian Aramaic*. Münster: Ugarit-Verlag.

Bhayro, Siam. 2013. 'The Reception of Mesopotamian and Early Jewish Traditions in the Aramaic Incantation Bowls'. *Aramaic Studies* 11: 187–196.

———. 2014 [2018]. 'A Jewish Aramaic Magic Bowl Containing the Formula of Ḥanina Ben Dosa, and the Problem of Psalm 24:8b in the Magic Bowls'. *Bulletin of the Asia Institute* 28: 121–126.

———. 2015. 'Divorcing a Demon: Incantation Bowls and BT Giṭṭin 85b'. In *The Archeology and Material Culture of the Babylonian Talmud*, edited by Markham J. Geller, 121–132. Leiden: Brill.

———. 2015. 'On Early Jewish Literature and the Aramaic Magic Bowls'. *Aramaic Studies* 13: 54–68.

———. 2017. 'An Aramaic Magic Bowl for Fertility and Success in Childbirth: Lisboa, Museu Da Farmácia (Lisbon, Pharmacy Museum), Inv. No. 10895'. *Aramaic Studies* 15 (1): 106–111.

———. 2020. 'Moses in the Aramaic Magic Bowls'. Paper presented at Magic in Late Antiquity conference, Hebrew University of Jerusalem, 1–3 March 2020).

———. 2021. 'The Use of Quotations from the Psalms in the Aramaic Magic Bowls'. In *You who live in the shelter of the Most High (Ps. 91:1): The Use of Psalms in Jewish and Christian*

Traditions, edited by Ida Fröhlich, Nora Dávid, and Gerhard Langer, 69–82. Göttingen: Vandenhoeck & Ruprecht.

Bhayro, Siam, James Nathan Ford, Dan Levene, and Ortal-Paz Saar. 2018. *Aramaic Magic Bowls in the Vorderasiatisches Museum in Berlin: Descriptive List and Edition of Selected Texts* Leiden: Brill.

Billiet, Joseph. 1931. 'La collection Lycklama au Musée de Cannes'. *Gazette des Beaux-Arts*, 828: 321–340.

Bohak, Gideon. 2008. *Ancient Jewish Magic: A History*. Cambridge: Cambridge University Press.

———. 2012. 'From Qumran to Cairo: The Lives and Times of a Jewish Exorcistic Formula (with an Appendix by Shaul Shaked)'. In *Ritual Healing: Magic, Ritual and Medical Therapy from Antiquity until the Early Modern Period*, edited by Ildikó Csepregi and Charles Burnett, 31–52. Florence: SISMEL Edizioni del Galluzzo.

Borobio, E. M. 2003. 'A Magical Bowl in Judaeo-Aramaic'. *Isimu* 6: 323–336.

Boyarin, Daniel. 1978. 'On the History of the Babylonian Jewish Aramaic Reading Traditions: The Reflexes of *a and *ā'. *Journal of Near Eastern Studies* 37 (2): 141–160.

Breuer, Yochanan. 2002. *The Hebrew in the Babylonian Talmud According to the Manuscripts of the Tractate Pesaḥim*. Jerusalem: Magnes Press. (Hebrew)

Brodie, Neil. 2008. 'The Market Background to the April 2003 Plunder of the Iraq National Museum'. In *The Destruction of Cultural Heritage in Iraq*, edited by Peter G. Stone and Joanne Farchakh Bajjaly, 41–54. Woodbridge: Boydell Press.

Chwolson, Daniel. 1882. 'Die Inschriften auf den babylonischen Thongefässen'. In *Corpus Inscriptionum Hebraicarum*, col. 103–120. St Petersburg: H. Schmitzdorff.

Cook, Edward M. 1992. 'An Aramaic Incantation Bowl from Khafaje'. *Bulletin of the American Schools of Oriental Research* 285: 79–81.

Díez Macho, Alejandro. 1958. "Onqelos Manuscript With Babylonian Transliterated Vocalization in the Vatican Library.' *Vetus Testamentum*, 8 (1): 113–133.

Driver, G.R. 1930. 'A Magic Bowl'. *Revue d'Assyriologie* 27: 61–64.

Elitzur, Yoel. 2013. 'Epigraphic Hebrew: Roman and Byzantine Period'. In *Encyclopedia of Hebrew Language and Linguistics*, edited by Geoffrey Khan Leiden: Brill. http://dx.doi.org/10.1163/2212-4241_ehll_EHLL_COM_00000257, accessed 27 March 2022.

Epstein, Ya'aḳov Naḥum. 1921. 'Gloses Babylo-Araméennes'. *Revue des études juives* 73: 27–58.

———. 1922. 'Gloses Babylo-Araméennes'. *Revue des études juives* 74: 40–72.

Fain, Tatyana, James Nathan Ford, and Alexey Lyavdansky. 2016. 'Aramaic Incantation Bowls at the State Hermitage Museum, St. Petersburg'. *Babel und Bibel* 9: 289–324.

Faraj, Ali H. 2010. *Coppe magiche dall'antico Iraq con testi in aramaico giudaico di età ellenistica*. Milan: Lampi di Stampa.

———. 2010. 'An Incantation Bowl of Biblical Verses and a Syriac Incantation Bowl for the Protection of a House'. In *Proceedings of the 13th Italian Meeting of Afro-Asiatic Linguistics,*

Held in Udine, May 21st-24th, 2007, edited by F.M. Fales and G.F. Grassi, 205–212. Padova: Sargon Editrice e Libreria.

———. 2021. 'Blessing for BYRKWBY Son of MYŠW – An Unedited Incantation Bowl from the Iraq Museum, IM 76752'. *ARAM* 33 (1/2): 289–294.

Faraj, Ali H., and Marco Moriggi. 2005. 'Two Incantation Bowls from the Iraq Museum (Baghdad)'. *Orientalia* 74: 71–82.

Fassberg, Steven E. 2013. 'Pausal Forms'. In *Encyclopedia of Hebrew Language and Linguistics*, edited by Geoffrey Khan. Leiden: Brill. http://dx.doi.org/10.1163/2212-4241_ehll_EHLL_COM_00000273, accessed 26 November 2021.

Ford, James Nathan. 2006. 'Review of Dan Levene, A Corpus of Magic Bowls: Incantation Texts in Jewish Aramaic from Late Antiquity'. *Journal of Semitic Studies* 51: 207–214.

———. 2011. 'A New Parallel to the Jewish Babylonian Aramaic Incantation Bowl IM 76106 (Nippur 11 N 78)'. *Aramaic Studies* 9 (2): 249–277.

———. 2012. 'Phonetic Spellings of the Subordinating Particle *d(y)* in the Jewish Babylonian Aramaic Magic Bowls'. *Aramaic Studies* 10 (2): 215–247.

———. 2014. 'Notes on Some Recently Published Magic Bowls in the Schøyen Collection and Two New Parallels'. *Aula Orientalis* 32 (2): 235–264.

———. 2016 'New Light from Babylonia on the Semamit Story'. *Eretz-Israel* 32: 149–161. (Hebrew)

Ford, James Nathan, and Alon Ten-Ami. 2011/12. 'An Incantation Bowl for Rav Mešaršia Son of Qaqay'. *Tarbiẓ* 80: 219–230.

Ford, James Nathan, and Dan Levene. 2012. '"For Aḥata-de-'abuh Daughter of Imma:" Two Aramaic Incantation Bowls in the Vorderasiatisches Museum, Berlin (VA 2414 and VA 2426)'. *Journal of Semitic Studies* 57 (1): 53–67.

Ford, James Nathan, and Matthew Morgenstern. 2020. *Aramaic Incantation Bowls in Museum Collections: The Frau Professor Hilprecht Collection of Babylonian Antiquities, Jena.* Leiden: Brill.

Franco, Fulvio. 1978/79. 'Five Aramaic Incantation Bowls from Tell Baruda (Choche)'. *Mesopotamia* 13–14: 233–249.

Frim, Daniel J. 2021. 'Hebrew in the Incantation Bowls and in the Babylonian Vocalization Tradition'. *Journal of Semitic Studies* 66 (1): 27–51.

Furley, William D. and Jan Maarten Bremer. 2001. *Greek Hymns*, vol. 1. Tübingen: Mohr Siebeck.

Gawlikowski, Michel. 1990. 'Une coupe magique araméenne'. *Semitica* 38: 137–145.

Geller, Markham J. 1976. 'Two Incantation Bowls Inscribed in Syriac and Aramaic'. *Bulletin of the School of Oriental and African Studies* 39: 422–427.

———. 1980. 'Four Aramaic Incantation Bowls'. In *The Bible World: Essays in Honor of Cyrus H. Gordon,* edited by Gary Rendsburg, Ruth Adler, Milton Arfa, and Nathan H. Winter, 47–60. New York: Ktav.

———. 1986. 'Eight Incantation Bowls'. *Orientalia Lovaniensia Periodica* 17: 101–117.

———. 1997 'More Magic Spells and Formulae'. *Bulletin of the School of Oriental and African Studies* 60: 327–335.

Golinets, Viktor. 2013. 'Masora, Tiberian.' In *Encyclopedia of Hebrew Language and Linguistics*, edited by Geoffrey Khan. Leiden: Brill, 2013. http://dx.doi.org/10.1163/2212-4241_ehll_EHLL_COM_00000191, accessed 26 November 2021.

Gordon, Cyrus H. 1934. 'Aramaic Magical Bowls in the Istanbul and Baghdad Museums'. *Archiv Orientální* 6: 319–334.

———. 1934. 'An Aramaic Exorcism'. *Archiv Orientální* 6: 466–474.

———. 1934. 'An Aramaic Incantation'. *The Annual of the American Schools of Oriental Research* 14: 141–144.

———. 1937. 'Aramaic and Mandaic Magical Bowls'. *Archiv Orientální* 9: 84–106.

———. 1941. 'Aramaic Incantation Bowls'. *Orientalia* 10: 116–141, 272–276, 278–289, 339–360.

———. 1951. 'Two Magic Bowls in Teheran'. *Orientalia* 20: 306–315.

———. 1978. 'Two Aramaic Incantations'. In *Biblical and Near Eastern Studies: Essays in Honor of William Sanford LaSor*, edited by Gary A. Tuttle, 231–244. Grand Rapids: Eerdmans.

———. 1984. 'Magic Bowls in the Moriah Collection'. *Orientalia* 53: 220–241.

Gordon, Richard. 2019. 'Imaginative Force and Verbal Energy in Latin Curse-Tablets'. In *Litterae Magicae: Studies in Honour of Roger S. O. Tomlin, vol. 2, edited by Celia Sánchez Natalías, 111–129. Zaragoza: Libros Pórtico.

Gorea, Maria. 2003. 'Trois nouvelles coupes magiques araméennes'. *Semitica* 51: 73–92.

Greenfield, Jonas C. 1973. 'Notes on Some Aramaic and Mandaic Magic Bowls'. *Journal of the Ancient Near Eastern Society of Columbia University* 5 (1): 149–156.

Gross, Simcha and Avigail Manekin-Bamberger. 2022. 'Babylonian Jewish Society: The Evidence of the Incantation Bowls'. *Jewish Quarterly Review* 112 (1): 1–30.

Halévy, Joseph. 1877. 'Observations sur un vase judéo-babylonien du British Museum'. *Comptes rendus des séances de l'académie des inscriptions et belles-lettres* 5: 288–293.

Harari, Yuval. 2017. *Jewish Magic before the Rise of Kabbalah*. Detroit: Wayne State University Press.

Harviainen, Tapani. 1981. 'An Aramaic Incantation Bowl from Borsippa: Another Specimen of Eastern Aramaic "Koiné"'. *Studia Orientalia* 51 (14): 3–28.

Herman, Geoffrey. 2019. 'Jewish Identity in Babylonia in the Period of the Incantation Bowls'. In *A Question of Identity: Social, Political, and Historical Aspects of Identity Dynamics in Jewish and Other Contexts*, edited by Dikla Rivlin Katz, Noah Hacham, Geoffrey Herman, and Lilach Sagiv, 131–152. Berlin: Walter de Gruyter.

———. 2021. 'In Search of Non-Rabbinic Judaism in Sasanian Babylonia'.In *Diversity and Rabbinization: Jewish Texts and Societies Between 400 and 1,000 CE*, edited by Gavin

McDowell, Ron Naiweld, and Daniel Stökl Ben Ezra, 121–137. Cambridge: Open Book Publishers.

———. 2021. 'An Unpublished Incantation Bowl with a Citation from Isaiah 40'. *Semitica* 63: 349–353.

Hickson, Frances V. 1993. *Roman Prayer Language: Livy and the Aeneid of Vergil.* Stuttgart: B.G. Teubner.

Hunter, Erica C. D. 2000. 'Two Incantation Bowls from Babylon'. *Iraq* 62: 139–147.

Hyvernat, Henri. 1885. 'Sur un vase judéo-babylonien du Musée Lycklama de Cannes (Provence)'. *Zeitschrift für Keilschriftforschung* 2: 113–148.

Isbell, Charles D. 1975. *Corpus of the Aramaic Incantation Bowls.* Missoula: Scholars Press.

———. 1976. 'Two New Aramaic Incantation Bowls'. *Bulletin of the American Schools of Oriental Research* 223: 15–23.

Jacobson, Joshua R. 2013. 'Biblical Accents: Cantillation'. In *Encyclopedia of Hebrew Language and Linguistics*, edited by Geoffrey Khan. Leiden: Brill. http://dx.doi.org/10.1163/2212- 4241_ehll_EHLL_COM_00000841, accessed 26 November 2021.

Jeruzalmi, Isak. 1963. 'Les coupes magiques araméennes de Mésopotamie'. PhD dissertation, Université de Paris.

Judge, E.A. 1987. 'The Magical Use of Scripture in the Papyri'. In *Perspectives on Language and Text: Essays and Poems in Honor of Francis I. Andersen's Sixtieth Birthday*, edited by Edgar Conrad and Edward Newing, 339–349. Winona Lake: Eisenbrauns.

Kaufman, Stephen A. 1973. 'A Unique Magic Bowl from Nippur'. *Journal of Near Eastern Studies* 32 (1/2): 170–174.

———. 1975. 'Appendix C: Alphabetic Texts'. In *Excavations at Nippur: Eleventh Season*, edited by McGuire Gibson, 151–152. Chicago: University of Chicago Press.

Khan, Geoffrey. 2013. 'Vocalization, Babylonian'. In *Encyclopedia of Hebrew Language and Linguistics*, edited by Geoffrey Khan. Leiden: Brill. http://dx.doi.org/10.1163/2212-4241_ehll_EHLL_COM_00000449, accessed 11 November 2021.

———. 2020. *The Tiberian Pronunciation Tradition of Biblical Hebrew*, vol. 1. Cambridge: Open Book Publishers.

Korsvoll, Nils H. 2018. 'Bible Bible Everywhere? Reviewing the Distribution of Biblical Quotes in Ancient Amulets'. *Biblische Notizen* 176: 89–110.

Kraus, Thomas J. 2007. 'Βους, Βαινχωωχ und Septuaginta-Psalm 90? Überlegungen zu den sogenannten "Bous"-Amuletten und dem beliebtesten Bibeltext für apotropäische Zwecke'. *Zeitschrift für Antikes Christentum* 11 (3): 479–491.

Kwasman, Theodore, and Christa Müller-Kessler. 2012. 'Once Again on the Unique Incantation Bowl BM 135563'. *Journal of the American Oriental Society* 132 (2): 189–198.

Lacau, Pierre. 1894. 'Une coupe d'incantation'. *Revue d'Assyriologie* 3 (2): 49–51.

Lanfer, Peter T. 2015. 'Why Biblical Scholars Should Study Aramaic Bowl Spells'. *Aramaic Studies* 13: 9–23.

Layard, Austen Henry. 1853. *Discoveries among the Ruins of Nineveh and Babylon*. New York: G. P. Putnam and Co.

Levene, Dan. 1999. '"... And by the Name of Jesus ...": An Unpublished Magic Bowl in Jewish Aramaic'. *Jewish Studies Quarterly* 6 (4): 283–308.

———. 2002. 'Curse or Blessing: What's in the Magic Bowl?' Parkes Institute Pamphlet No. 2. Southampton.

———. 2003. *A Corpus of Magic Bowls: Incantation Texts in Jewish Aramaic from Late Antiquity*. London: Kegan Paul.

———. 2003. 'Heal O' Israel: A Pair of Duplicate Magic Bowls from the Pergamon Museum in Berlin'. *Journal of Jewish Studies* 54 (1): 104–121.

———. 2005. 'Jewish Liturgy and Magic Bowls'. In *Studies in Jewish Prayer*, edited by Robert Hayward and Brad Embry, 163–184. Oxford: Oxford University Press.

———. 2007. '"If You Appear as a Pig:" Another Incantation Bowl (Moussaieff 164)'. *Journal of Semitic Studies* 52 (1): 59–70.

———. 2013. *Jewish Aramaic Curse Texts from Late-Antique Mesopotamia: 'May These Curses Go Out and Flee'*. Leiden: Brill.

Levene, Dan, and Siam Bhayro. 2005/6. '"Bring to the Gates ... upon a Good Smell and upon Good Fragrances:" An Aramaic Incantation Bowl for Success in Business'. *Archiv Für Orientforschung* 51: 242–246.

Levene, Dan, and Gideon Bohak. 2012. 'A Babylonian Jewish Aramaic Incantation Bowl with a List of Deities and Toponyms'. *Jewish Studies Quarterly* 19: 56–72.

Levene, Dan, Dalia Marx, and Siam Bhayro. 2014. '"Gabriel Is on Their Right:" Angelic Protection in Jewish Magic and Babylonian Lore'. *Studia Mesopotamica* 1: 185–198.

Manekin-Bamberger, Avigail. 2015. 'Jewish Legal Formulae in the Aramaic Incantation Bowls'. *Aramaic Studies* 13: 69–81.

———. 2018. 'Intersections between Law and Magic in Ancient Jewish Texts'. PhD dissertation, Tel Aviv University. (Hebrew)

———. 2020. 'Who Were the Jewish "Magicians: behind the Aramaic Incantation Bowls?' *Journal of Jewish Studies* 71 (2): 235-254.

McCullough, William Stewart. 1967. *Jewish and Mandaean Incantation Bowls in the Royal Ontario Museum*. Toronto: University of Toronto Press.

Misgav, Haggai. 2018. 'Jewish-Aramaic Incantation Bowls'. In *Finds Gone Astray: ADCA Confiscated Items*, edited by Dalit Regev and Hananya Hizmi, 53–72. Jerusalem: The Antiquities Department of the Civil Administration.

Mishor, Mordechai. 2007. 'Hebrew in the Babylonian Incantation Bowls'. In *Sha'arei Lashon: Studies in Hebrew, Aramaic and Jewish Languages Presented to Moshe Bar-Asher*, vol. 2, edited by Aharon Maman, Steven E. Fassberg, and Yohanan Breuer, 204–227. Jerusalem: Bialik Institute. (Hebrew)

Molin, Dorota. 2017. 'The Language of the Biblical Hebrew Quotations in the Aramaic Incantation Bowls'. MA thesis, University of Cambridge.

———. 2020. 'Biblical Quotations in the Aramaic Incantation Bowls and Their Contribution to the Study of the Babylonian Reading Tradition'. In *Studies in Semitic Vocalisation and Reading Traditions*, edited by Aaron D. Hornkohl and

Geoffrey Khan, 147–170. Cambridge: Open Book Publishers.

———. 2021. 'The Jewish Neo-Aramaic Dialect of Dohok: A Comparative Perspective'. PhD dissertation, University of Cambridge.

Montgomery, James A. 1913. *Aramaic Incantation Texts from Nippur.* Philadelphia: University of Pennsylvania: The Museum.

Morgenstern, Matthew. 2004. 'Notes on a Recently Published Aramaic Magic Bowl'. *Aramaic Studies* 2 (2): 207–222.

———. 2007. 'The Jewish Babylonian Aramaic Magic Bowl BM 91767 Reconsidered'. *Le Muséon* 120: 5–27.

Moriggi, Marco. 2005. 'Two New Incantation Bowls from Rome (Italy).' *Aramaic Studies* 3: 43–58.

Morony, Michael G. 2003. 'Magic and Society in Late Sasanian Iraq'. In *Prayer, Magic, and the Stars in the Ancient and Late Antique World,* edited by Scott Noegel, Joel Walker, and Brannon Wheeler, 83–107. University Park: Pennsylvania State University Press.

———. 2007. 'Religion and the Aramaic Incantation Bowls'. *Religion Compass* 1 (4): 414–429.

Müller-Kessler, Christa. 1994. 'Eine aramaische Zauberschale im Museum für Vor- und Fruhgeschichte zu Berlin'. *Orientalia* 63: 5–9.

———. 2001. 'Die Zauberschalensammlung des British Museum'. *Archiv für Orientforschung* 48/49: 115–145.

———. 2005. *Die Zauberschalentexte in der Hilprecht-Sammlung, Jena, und weitere Nippur-Texte anderer Sammlungen*. Wiesbaden: Harrassowitz.

———. 2013. 'The Use of Biblical Quotations in Jewish Aramaic Incantation Bowls'. In *Studies in Magic and Divination in the Biblical World*, edited by Helen R. Jacobus, Anne Katrine de Hemmer Gudme, and Philippe Guillaume, 225–240. Piscataway: Gorgias Press.

———. 2013. 'Eine ungewöhnliche Hekhalot-Zauberschale und ihr babylonisches Umfeld: Jüdisches Gedankengut in den Magischen Texten des Ostens'. *Frankfurter Judaistische Beiträge* (38): 69–84.

———. 2017. 'Zauberschalen und ihre Umwelt: Ein Überblick über das Schreibmedium Zauberschale'. In *Zauber und Magie im antiken Palästina und in seiner Umwelt*, edited by Jens Kamlah, Rolf Schäfer, and Markus Witte, 59–94. Wiesbaden: Harrassowitz.

Müller-Kessler, Christa, and Theodore Kwasman. 2000. 'A Unique Talmudic Aramaic Incantation Bowl'. *Journal of the American Oriental Society* 120 (2): 159–165.

Myhrman, David W. 1909. 'An Aramaic Incantation Text'. In *Hilprecht Anniversary Volume: Studies in Assyriology and Archaeology Dedicated to Hermann V. Hilprecht upon the Twenty-Fifth Anniversary of His Doctorate and His Fiftieth Birthday (July 28)*, 342–351. Leipzig: J.C. Hinrichs.

Narquis, M. 1934. 'An Aramaic Incantation'. *Tarbiẓ* 6: 106–107.

Naveh, Joseph, and Shaul Shaked. 1987. *Amulets and Magic Bowls: Aramaic Incantations of Late Antiquity*, 2nd ed. Jerusalem: Magnes Press.

———. 1993. *Magic Spells and Formulae: Aramaic Incantations of Late Antiquity*. Jerusalem: Magnes Press.

Obermann, Julian. 1940. 'Two Magic Bowls: New Incantation Texts from Mesopotamia'. *The American Journal of Semitic Languages and Literature* 57: 1–31.

Ofer, Yosef. 'Masora, Babylonian'. 2013. In *Encyclopedia of Hebrew Language and Linguistics*, edited by Geoffrey Khan. Leiden: Brill. http://dx.doi.org/10.1163/2212-4241_ehll_EHLL_COM_00000613, accessed 24 November 2021.

Polzer, Natalie C. 1986. 'The Bible in the Aramaic Magic Bowls'. PhD dissertation, McGill University.

Pickering, S.R. 1999. 'The Significance of Non-Continuous New Testament Textual Materials in Papyri'. In *Studies in the Early Text of the Gospels and Acts*, edited by David G.K. Taylor, 121–141. Atlanta: SBL.

Rebiger, Bill. 2003. 'Die magische Verwendung von Psalmen im Judentum'. In *Ritual und Poesie: Formen und Orte religiöser Dichtung im alten Orient, im Judentum und im Christentum*, edited by Erich Zenger, 265–281. Freiburg: Herder.

Reif, Stefan C. 2017. 'Liturgy as an Educational Process in Talmudic and Medieval Judaism'. In *Jewish Education from Antiquity to the Middle Ages: Studies in Honour of Philip S. Alexander*, edited by George R. Brooke and Renate Smithius, 252–268. Leiden: Brill.

Rosenthal, D. 1982. 'Ḥazal ve-Ḥilufei Nusaḥ ha-Miqra'. In *Sefer Yiṣḥaq 'Aryeh Zeligman: Ma'amarim ba-Miqra' u-va-'Olam he-'Atiq* vol. 2, edited by Yair Zakovitch and Alexander Rofe, 402–417. Jerusalem: Rubinstein.

Saar, Ortal-Paz. 2013. 'An Incantation Bowl for Sowing Discord'. *Journal of Semitic Studies* 58 (2): 241–56.

Salzer, Dorothea M. 2010. *Die Magie der Anspielung: Form und Funktion der biblischen Anspielungen in den magischen Texten der Kairoer Geniza*. Tübingen: Mohr Siebeck.

Sanzo, Joseph E. 2014. *Scriptural Incipits on Amulets from Late Antique Egypt: Text, Typology, and Theory*. Tübingen: Mohr Siebeck.

Schäfer, Peter. 1996. 'Jewish Liturgy and Magic'. In *Geschichte – Tradition – Reflexion: Festschrift für Martin Hengel zum 70*, edited by Hubert Cancik, Hermann Lichtenberger, and Peter Schäfer, 541–556. Tübingen: J.C.B. Mohr.

Schäfer, Peter and Shaul Shaked. 1994–1999. *Magische Texte aus der Kairoer Geniza*, 3 vols. Tübingen: Mohr Siebeck.

Schiffman, Lawrence H., and Michael D. Swartz. 1992. *Hebrew and Aramaic Incantation Texts from the Cairo Genizah: Selected Texts from Taylor-Schechter Box Kl*. Sheffield: JSOT Press.

Schwab, Moïse. 1886. 'Une coupe d'incantation'. *Revue d'Assyriologie* 1: 117–119.

———. 1891. 'Coupes à inscriptions magiques'. *Proceedings of the Society for Biblical Archaeology* 13 (1891), 583–595.

———. 1892. 'Deux vases judéo-babyloniens'. *Revue d'Assyriologie* 2: 136–142.

———. 1916. 'Amulets and Bowls with Magic Inscriptions'. *Jewish Quarterly Review* 7: 619–628.

Segal, J. B. 2000. *Catalogue of the Aramaic and Mandaic Incantation Bowls in the British Museum*. London: British Museum Press.

Shaked, Shaul. 1995. '"Peace Be Upon You, Exalted Angels:" On Hekhalot, Liturgy, and Incantation Bowls'. *Jewish Studies Quarterly* 2: 197–219.

———. 1999. 'The Poetics of Spells: Language and Structure in Aramaic Incantations of Late Antiquity, 1: The Divorce Formula and Its Ramifications'. In *Mesopotamian Magic: Textual, Historical, and Interpretative Perspectives*, edited by Tzvi Abusch and Karel van der Toorn, 173–195. Groningen: Styx Publications.

———. 2005. 'Form and Purpose in Aramaic Spells: Some Jewish Themes'. In *Officina Magica: Essays on the Practice of Magic in Antiquity*, edited by Shaul Shaked, 1–30. Leiden: Brill.

———. 2006. 'Dramatis Personae in the Jewish Magic Texts: Some Differences Between Incantation Bowls and Geniza Magic'. *Jewish Studies Quarterly* 13 (4): 363–387.

———. 2011. 'Transmission and Transformation of Spells: The Case of the Jewish Babylonian Aramaic Bowls'. In *Continuity and Innovation in the Magical Tradition*, edited by Gideon Bohak, Yuval Harari, and Shaul Shaked, 187–217. Leiden: Brill.

———. 2015. 'Rabbis in Incantation Bowls'. In *The Archeology and Material Culture of the Babylonian Talmud*, edited by Markham J. Geller, 97–120. Leiden: Brill.

Shaked, Shaul, James Nathan Ford, and Siam Bhayro. 2013. *Aramaic Bowl Spells: Jewish Babylonian Aramaic Bowls*, vol. 1. Leiden: Brill.

———. 2022. *Aramaic Bowl Spells: Jewish Babylonian Aramaic Bowls*, vol. 2. Leiden: Brill.

Smelik, K.A.D. 1978. 'An Aramaic Incantation Bowl in the Allard Pierson Museum'. *Bibliotheca Orientalis* 35: 174–177.

Sperber, Alexander. 2004. *The Bible in Aramaic: Based on Old Manuscripts and Printed Texts*, vols. I–III. Leiden: Brill.

van der Vliet, Jacques. 2011. 'Literature, Liturgy, Magic: A Dynamic Continuum'. In *Christianity in Egypt: Literary Production and Intellectual Trends*, edited by Paola Buzi and Alberto Camplani, 555–574. Rome: Institutum Patristicum Augustinianum.

Yamauchi, Edwin. 1965. 'Aramaic Magic Bowls'. *Journal of the American Oriental Society* 85 (4): 511–523.

Yeivin, Israel. 1985. *The Tradition of Hebrew as Reflected by Babylonian Vocalization*, 2 vols. Jerusalem: Hebrew Language Academy Press. (Hebrew)

Zenger, Erich. 2000. 'Psalm 91'. In *Psalmen 51-100*, edited by Frank-Lothar Hossfeld and Erich Zenger. Freiburg: Herder.

ANCIENT SOURCES INDEX

For a complete list of incantation bowl texts in the Catalogue, see the Table of Distribution.

Hebrew Bible
(Introduction)

Gen. 21.1	26	Isa. 60.6	28
Gen. 25.21	26	Isa. 60.8	28
Gen. 30.22	24–26	Isa. 60.11	28
Exod. 3.14	11–12	Jer. 8.4	18
Exod. 14.31	22	Amos 8.14	18
Exod. 15.3	21	Zech. 3.2	12, 22, 23–24
Exod. 15.7	24		
Exod. 15.15	38	Ps. 10.16	11, 21
Exod. 15.16	20	Ps. 24.8	11, 21
Exod. 15.18	11, 21	Ps. 55.9	17
Exod. 22.23	29	Ps. 69.24	29, 38
Lev. 6.5	29	Ps. 69.26	29
Lev. 6.6	29	Ps. 72.18–19	6
Lev. 9.24	29	Ps. 89.53	6
Lev. 26.29	29, 33	Ps. 91.1	17, 22, 25, 35–36
Lev. 26.37	18		
Num. 6.24–26	23	Ps. 93.1	11, 21
Num. 9.23	22	Ps. 104.20	14
Num. 10.35	17–18, 34	Ps. 104.31	6
Num. 15.37–41	26	Ps. 106.47	6
Deut. 6.4	17, 22, 26	Ps. 106.48	6
Deut. 6.4–9	6, 26	Ps. 115.1	9, 15–16
Deut. 6.19	28–29	Prov. 3.4	27
Deut. 11.13–21	6, 26		
Deut. 28.22	19, 29		
Deut. 28.28	19, 29		
Deut. 28.35	19, 29		
Deut. 28.57	36–37		
Deut. 29.19	29		
Isa. 40.12	14–15		
Isa. 45.2	10–11		

Incantation Bowls (Introduction)

A 33965	13
AMB 3	17–18, 34–35
AMB 9	9, 18, 19, 29, 33–34, 38
AMB 11	17
AMB 12b	15
AMB 13	24
HS 3027	13
HS 3030	13
IM 141803	13, 38
JBA 9	14, 21
JBA 28	11
JBA 46	36–37
JBA 55	17
M 108	6–7, 14
M 155	10–11
MFL 10895	24–25
MS 1927/2:5	27
MS 2053/159	20–21
SD 34	27–28
VA 2423	35–36
VA 2484	28–29
VA 3853	6
VA 3854	6

Amulets and Genizah Texts

T-S K 1.143	26
T-S K 1.157	26

Rabbinic Texts

Seder ʿAmram	6, 117, 133, 135, 141, 142, 152
Sifre Num. 40	23
m. Šebu. 4.13	64, 100, 138, 144, 151

Targumim (Introduction)

Tg. Ps-J.	23

Cambridge Semitic Languages and Cultures

General Editor Geoffrey Khan

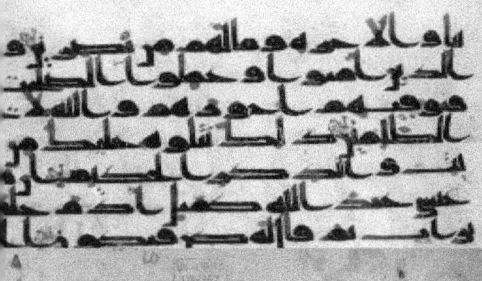

Cambridge Semitic Languages and Cultures

About the series

This series is published by Open Book Publishers in collaboration with the Faculty of Asian and Middle Eastern Studies of the University of Cambridge. The aim of the series is to publish in open-access form monographs in the field of Semitic languages and the cultures associated with speakers of Semitic languages. It is hoped that this will help disseminate research in this field to academic researchers around the world and also open up this research to the communities whose languages and cultures the volumes concern. This series includes philological and linguistic studies of Semitic languages, editions of Semitic texts, and studies of Semitic cultures. Titles in the series will cover all periods, traditions and methodological approaches to the field. The editorial board comprises Geoffrey Khan, Aaron Hornkohl, and Esther-Miriam Wagner.

This is the first Open Access book series in the field; it combines the high peer-review and editorial standards with the fair Open Access model offered by OBP. Open Access (that is, making texts free to read and reuse) helps spread research results and other educational materials to everyone everywhere, not just to those who can afford it or have access to well-endowed university libraries.

Copyrights stay where they belong, with the authors. Authors are encouraged to secure funding to offset the publication costs and thereby sustain the publishing model, but if no institutional funding is available, authors are not charged for publication. Any grant secured covers the actual costs of publishing and is not taken as profit. In short: we support publishing that respects the authors and serves the public interest.

UNIVERSITY OF
CAMBRIDGE
Faculty of Asian and Middle Eastern Studies

You can find more information about this serie at:
http://www.openbookpublishers.com/section/107/1

Other titles in the series

Studies in the Masoretic Tradition of the Hebrew Bible
Daniel J. Crowther, Aaron D. Hornkohl and Geoffrey Khan

https://doi.org/10.11647/OBP.0330

Diachronic Variation in the Omani Arabic Vernacular of the Al-ʿAwābī District
From Carl Reinhardt (1894) to the Present Day

Roberta Morano

https://doi.org/10.11647/OBP.0298

Sefer ha-Pardes by Jedaiah ha-Penini
A Critical Edition with English Translation

David Torollo

https://doi.org/10.11647/OBP.0299

Neo-Aramaic and Kurdish Folklore from Northern Iraq
A Comparative Anthology with a Sample of Glossed Texts, Volume 1

Geoffrey Khan, Masoud Mohammadirad, Dorota Molin & Paul M. Noorlander

https://doi.org/10.11647/OBP.0306

Neo-Aramaic and Kurdish Folklore from Northern Iraq
A Comparative Anthology with a Sample of Glossed Texts, Volume 2

Geoffrey Khan, Masoud Mohammadirad, Dorota Molin & Paul M. Noorlander

https://doi.org/10.11647/OBP.0307

The Neo-Aramaic Oral Heritage of the Jews of Zakho
Oz Aloni

https://doi.org/10.11647/OBP.0272

Points of Contact
The Shared Intellectual History of Vocalisation in Syriac, Arabic, and Hebrew

Nick Posegay

🏆 Winner of the British and Irish Association of Jewish Studies (BIAJS) Annual Book Prize

https://https://doi.org/10.11647/OBP.0271

A Handbook and Reader of Ottoman Arabic
Esther-Miriam Wagner (ed.)

https://doi.org/10.11647/OBP.0208

Diversity and Rabbinization
Jewish Texts and Societies between 400 and 1000 CE

Gavin McDowell, Ron Naiweld, Daniel Stökl Ben Ezra (eds)

https://doi.org/10.11647/OBP.0219

New Perspectives in Biblical and Rabbinic Hebrew
Aaron D. Hornkohl and Geoffrey Khan (eds)

https://doi.org/10.11647/OBP.0250

The Marvels Found in the Great Cities and in the Seas and on the Islands
A Representative of 'Aǧā'ib Literature in Syriac

Sergey Minov

https://doi.org/10.11647/OBP.0237

Studies in the Grammar and Lexicon of Neo-Aramaic
Geoffrey Khan and Paul M. Noorlander (eds)

https://doi.org/10.11647/OBP.0209

Jewish-Muslim Intellectual History Entangled
Textual Materials from the Firkovitch Collection, Saint Petersburg

Camilla Adang, Bruno Chiesa, Omar Hamdan, Wilferd Madelung, Sabine Schmidtke and Jan Thiele (eds)

https://doi.org/10.11647/OBP.0214

Studies in Semitic Vocalisation and Reading Traditions
Aaron Hornkohl and Geoffrey Khan (eds)

https://doi.org/10.11647/OBP.0207

Studies in Rabbinic Hebrew
Shai Heijmans (ed.)

https://doi.org/10.11647/OBP.0164

The Tiberian Pronunciation Tradition of Biblical Hebrew
Volume 1

Geoffrey Khan

🐂 *Winner of the 2021 Frank Moore Cross Book Award for best book related to the history and/or religion of the ancient Near East and Eastern Mediterranean*

https://doi.org/10.11647/OBP.0163

The Tiberian Pronunciation Tradition of Biblical Hebrew
Volume 2

Geoffrey Khan

🐂 *Winner of the 2021 Frank Moore Cross Book Award for best book related to the history and/or religion of the ancient Near East and Eastern Mediterranean*

https://doi.org/10.11647/OBP.0194

www.ingramcontent.com/pod-product-compliance
Lightning Source LLC
Chambersburg PA
CBHW040624240426
43666CB00020BA/2914